ACCLAIM FOR DR. JOE WENKE'S

YOU GOT TO BE KIDDING!

"A radically funny book." *Christopher Rudolph, The Advocate*

"Gisele, the notable transgender fashion model, graces the cover. And that image alone challenges the Bible. A transgender woman in a religious pose. . . . Get [You Got to be Kidding!] on your Kindle or take it on a trip, the time will fly by—boring this is not!"

Transgenderzone

"A riotously funny read, I recommend it to anyone who's ever questioned organised religion, especially that of the Bible-bashing, homophobic kind." *Anna, Look!*

"This is hilarious! Joe Wenke gives a nod to Mark Twain as he looks at the Bible with fresh eyes and with the pen of a thinking comic."

Bill Baker

"This is without a doubt the funniest book I've ever read. I sat with my parents and read aloud some of the passages and we all laughed a lot!"

Emma Charlton, Bookswithemma

"Very tongue-in-cheek, sarcastic and pointed, dedicated to Christopher Hitchens and Thomas Paine, both of whom would, I believe, really enjoy this book!" *Sarah Hulcey*

"The cover of the book itself is a slap in the face of tra~~~hobia. . . . If this book accomplishes on␣␣␣␣␣␣␣␣␣␣␣␣␣␣␣␣␣␣␣ced people toward acceptance of LGBT␣␣␣␣␣␣␣␣␣␣␣␣␣␣␣␣␣␣␣␣␣␣

Is␣␣␣␣␣␣␣␣␣␣␣␣␣␣␣␣␣␣␣␣␣ng & Wine

"Brave, brilliant and funny. Page after page, biblical chapter after biblical chapter, absurdity after absurdity, this book delivers laugh after laugh. Joe Wenke has crafted the answer to the fundamentalist literal reading of the Bible with the perfect recipe of rationality, candor and humor."

Max Gelt

"Brilliant . . . for once a funny look at ALL the Bible's insanity."

Jo Bryant

"Would make a really wicked Christmas present for your Christian friends who have a sense of humor and a sense of the ridiculous."

Ed Buckner, American Atheists

"Whether you are an atheist or a Christian who can see the absurdity of some of the anecdotes narrated in Holy Scripture, Joe Wenke's humor won't be wasted on you."

Mina's Bookshelf

"Oh my! This is very funny . . . Joe turns everything on its head and makes it a really interesting read."

Stephen Ormsby

"Great book! Funny and easy to read."

Violets and Tulips

"Funny and to the point read. Takes a look at the Bible and points out all sorts of inaccuracies, illogical stories and questions. Strongly recommend."

Hertzey

"Witty and wise. Joe Wenke takes a critical, provocative look at The Bible and he does so with regular hilarity."

Dana Hislop

"A must-read for anyone who still thinks the Bible is the inviolable word of God—sense of humor mandatory."

K. Sozaeva

"Deliciously witty!"

Jack Scott

"Such a funny read, my son & I actually read it together! Laughter abounds!"   *Rael*

"Irreverent and hilarious. I am no Bible scholar, but I feel like I have been given the funniest crib notes on this most widely read and probably as widely misunderstood book of all time. I laughed out loud at Wenke's common sense observations and interpretations of this tome."

Lorna Lee

"Entertaining and enlightening."   *Patti Bray*

"Will keep any freethinking reader laughing the whole way through."

George Lichman

"You will be laughing yourself silly while reading this book! In fact, you may find yourself bookmarking a bunch of pages to discuss with your pastor and friends later!"   *S. Henke*

"Twisted with humor, straight language and a little sarcasm, this personal theology is both provoking and entertaining."

Henk-Jan Van Der Klis

"This author allows the reader to explore and learn about the Bible with a tongue-in-cheek attitude that keeps you laughing and turning the pages."   *Tricia Schneider*

"Some of it made me feel like I might wind up in hell for reading it, but if you keep an open mind and a light heart, you'll have a blast."

Jon Yost

"I could not put this book down."   *Jackie Hepton*

"Don't read the Bible! Read this!"   *Dr. Dan*

YOU GOT TO BE KIDDING!

A Radical Satire of *The Bible*

A Radical Satire of *The Bible*

Stamford, Connecticut

2012

You Got To Be Kidding! A Radical Satire of The Bible

Trans Über LLC
www.transuber.com

To reach the author or Trans Über email: josephwenke@msn.com

ISBN: 978-0-9859002-0-5

Digital editions available.

Manufactured in the United States of America
Third Edition

Cover design: BlueMountainMarketing.com
Model: Gisele Xtravaganza
Photography: Nina Poon

www.joewenke.org
Follow Dr. Joe Wenke on twitter @joewenke.

For Thomas Paine and Christopher Hitchens

For Gisele Xtravaganza

Gisele, as a transgender woman, you have always stood up for the rights and dignity of gay, lesbian and transgender people. Now, as the angelic nun on the cover of my book, you again take a stand in support of freedom and equality, for your beatific image is itself a repudiation of Bible-backed bigotry. Thank you, Gisele, for being on the cover of my book. You are the best—beautiful, brilliant and brave.

Biographical Note: Gisele Xtravaganza is a successful high fashion model, actress, painter, event producer, legendary ballroom personality and transgender activist. During her modeling career she has worked with such professionals as Patricia Field, Patrick Demarchelier, Terry Richardson, Danielle Levitz, Jared Leto and many others. Her runway work includes The Blondes, Nico and Adrian. She has appeared in national magazines such as Interview, Out, Candy, Amelie G, Flaunt and many others. Gisele appeared in the movie The Extra Man with Katie Holmes, Kevin Kline, John C. Reilly and Paul Dano. She was also featured in the documentary Lost in the Crowd by Susi Graf. Gisele grew up in Harlem and attended the Harvey Milk High School.

CONTENTS

The Old Testament

The New Testament

THE OLD TESTAMENT

1

ADAM AND EVE

God is looking for Adam and Eve. They both ate a piece of fruit, and he is really pissed.

They're hiding behind some trees in the garden and are looking at their genitals, which they had never really noticed before. For some reason God is having a hard time finding Adam and Eve. "Where are you?" he cries out.

Adam decides to let God know where they are, figuring I suppose that he would eventually find them anyway. God is immediately in Adam's face, really upset about the fact that he and Eve ate the fruit. "Have you eaten of the tree of which I commanded you not to eat?" he says.

Cornered, Adam puts most of the blame on Eve, but implies that it's sort of God's fault too since creating Eve was his idea. He says, "The woman whom you gave to be with me, she gave me fruit of the tree and I ate."

God ignores Adam for the moment at least and turns on Eve. "What is it that you have done?" he says.

Eve will take none of the blame either. "The serpent deceived me, and I ate," she says. So now the serpent's in trouble, and God really throws the book at him. "Because you have done this," God says, "cursed are you above all livestock, and above all beasts in the field; on your belly shall you go."

I don't know how the serpent got around previously—whether it had legs or wings or whatever, but from now on it has to crawl. That's a tough punishment. But God is just getting started here. Before he's done, he makes sure that childbirth will be excruciating for Eve and all future women, and he makes Adam her boss. In fact, he makes men the boss of women forever more. For his part, Adam is going to have to work his ass off to even feed himself. His whole life is going to be miserable. Eve's too—nothing but misery and suffering. And at the end of it all they die. But here's the kicker: Everybody else who is ever going to be born gets the same punishment—work your ass off your whole miserable, god-forsaken life and then die.

If you ever find yourself wondering why life really sucks—like what's the story, why does it have to be this way, I just told you. And now that you know, there's really only one thing you can say and that is "Thank you, Lord."

2

CAIN AND ABEL

Right away things go from bad to worse.

Adam and Eve have two sons, Cain and Abel. The boys both want to get on God's good side, so they give him presents. Cain gives God a kind of fruit basket, and Abel gives him a sheep. God likes the sheep and hates the fruit basket. Cain should have known that God is very touchy when it comes to fruit. In any event, Cain takes all of this really badly and goes off and kills Abel, which is arguably the biggest overreaction to rejection in all of human history.

3

NOAH'S ARK

The generations pass, and nothing is working out as far as God is concerned. Just about everybody is behaving badly. There is corruption all around. You get the impression that there was nothing but sex and violence going on 24/7. God gets fed up and wants a do over. So he decides to kill everybody—not just the adults but infants and children too—and start from scratch. Even the animals have to go, although it isn't clear what they did to deserve the death penalty. I assume they were just acting like animals.

God's method is pretty smart, though. He decides to make it rain every single day until the earth is totally flooded, and everybody and everything drowns. Coincidentally this all takes forty days and forty nights. The one flaw I see in God's plan is that the fish should still be able to do OK in a flood since they can swim, although the salt water from all of the oceans getting into all of the rivers would probably cause big problems for the freshwater fish.

God's decision to flood the entire earth and kill everybody and everything is without a doubt far and away the greatest single act of genocide in the history of the world. It makes you wonder what God thought of the pathetic attempts of Hitler, Stalin and Mao to compete in the genocidal sweepstakes. They may have slaughtered millions, but there were still plenty of people left when they were done. God, however, has his eyes set on just one guy, Noah. Noah was the only guy that God thought was any good. He was so good God even gave his family a pass as well.

Noah was lucky in another way. Not only was he the one guy that God liked enough to spare, he was almost certainly the only guy at that time who was living in the middle of the desert and who had the amazing prescience to learn how to build a boat. So when God tells him to build a huge boat, an ark, Noah is ready.

Now the boat is big, at least for those days. Measured in feet, it was about 45-feet high, 75-feet wide, and 450-feet long. That's big, but hardly big enough to accommodate Noah, his family, all of the necessary supplies for more than a month at sea and, yes, at least two of every living species on earth and whatever it is they might need to survive (God actually tells Noah to bring seven pairs of all of the clean animals and birds and just a pair of all of the unclean animals--I hope that he could tell the difference because I certainly can't).

Scientists have identified more than one million species on earth, not including plants, and they estimate that there are millions more, like maybe more than eight million. Only God would know the total number. For the ark to accommodate at least two of every living thing on earth, giving everybody on it a little breathing room and making sure that there was proper segregation of predators and prey (though I'm not sure then what the predators eat, if not their prey), it would have to be really, really big. It's just a guess, but I'm thinking something along the lines of the state of Rhode Island.

There's also the question of how Noah rounded up all of the disparate and far-flung species, marooned as he was in the Middle East and without any real means of transportation. For example, who went out and picked up the polar bears and penguins? Where was the nearest elephant? And what about the kangaroos and kiwis?

Then there is the question of scale. There are some tiny creatures out there. Did Noah welcome on board all of the insects? Or was there a cut off? Did roaches and mosquitoes make it? How about bed bugs? And how about the worm that was just discovered living in the lungs of a lizard? I also find myself wondering how Noah and his family avoided stepping on all of those insects as they walked about the ark. No matter how careful they were, it must have gotten pretty crunchy at times.

Postscript to the story of Noah's Ark: Imagine the surprise of those unlucky animals, which after surviving the horrific flood were grabbed by Noah as they left the boat and were sacrificed to God in thanksgiving. This was a pretty big sacrifice since we are told that "some of every clean animal and of every clean bird" were sacrificed to an appreciative God. It sort of gives a whole new meaning to the idea that it ain't over 'til it's over.

Second Postscript to the story of Noah's Ark: Does anybody have any information on the bathroom situation on the ark? I have to confess. I don't really want to think about it, but it is an obvious issue.

4

THE TOWER OF BABEL

It should not be that surprising that God would have some amazing qualities. After all, he is God. But who would expect him to have such a wonderful sense of humor? Take the Tower of Babel story as one example. At this time, we are told that everybody on earth speaks the same language. I have no idea what this language was, but anyway everybody speaks it. Then a bunch of very clever people somehow build a very impressive city that includes the very first skyscraper—the Tower of Babel.

God gets wind of all this and decides to stop by and check it out. He sees what the people have done and what they might be capable of doing and decides to fuck with them. "Behold," he says, "They are one people, and they have all one language, and this is only the beginning of what they will do. And nothing they propose to do will be impossible for them." To cut them down to size, he kicks everybody out of the city, sends them scrambling across the face of the earth and instantaneously creates countless new languages, so nobody can understand what anybody else is saying.

You think you can accomplish great things, says God. Think again. The next time you open your mouth, nobody will have a fucking idea what you're saying. Now that's funny.

5

ABRAHAM AND THE COVENANT OF CIRCUMCISION

This may not seem like as big a deal as the whole Adam and Eve thing or Noah's ark, but it shows how weird God is. God sort of has guys that he sponsors. Noah was his guy, and Abraham was his guy too. Later on, it's Moses, and then, of course, Jesus, the ultimate guy, because he was God's only son—and God, too, which is extremely confusing, and of course it only gets more confusing when you add in the Holy Spirit, who's sort of like a bird—but anyway, I digress. The point is that Abraham was God's guy, but Abraham was always upset about the fact that he couldn't get his extraordinarily beautiful wife Sarah, pregnant. But God always reassured Abraham. He told him not to worry. God had Abraham pegged to be the father of nations.

Now it took God a long time to make good on this promise. Abraham was 99 years old when God finally got around to cutting a deal with him. But here's what's strange. When God finally tells Abraham that he will be the father of nations and any time he even looks at a woman, she will be impregnated, he decides that the sacred sign of this great covenant will be—a circumcised penis.

So that very day, Abraham runs out and has the tip of his penis cut off, and he grabs his son, Ishmael (born of the servant, Hagar), and has him circumcised too. He even circumcises all of his male slaves. All of this cutting of foreskin was to close his deal with God. And this is where once again you have to hand it to God. He keeps coming up with this stuff way out of left field. Yes, I'll make a deal with you, he says, but to seal it, I want you to cut off the tip of your dick. A simple handshake? I don't think so.

6

SODOM AND GOMORRAH

Here we go again. It's party time day and night in Sodom and Gomorrah, and God wants to put a stop to it. Once again there is just one good guy, in this case, Lot, and God plans on sparing him. He sends two angels to Lot's house, and Lot invites them to spend the night. In a rather shocking display of depravity, when the party animals of Sodom find out that angels are staying at Lot's house, they show up and demand that Lot turn the angels over to them so that they can fuck them up the ass. That's right. The guys from Sodom want to sodomize the angels. However, Lot, the good guy, has a rather shocking response of his own. His idea of saving the day is to offer his two virgin daughters to the crowd if they promise not to rape his angel guests, knowing, I guess, that the crowd swings both ways. The angels, of course, have God on their side, so they're never really in any danger. In fact, they're the ones who have been sent to destroy the town. They strike the would-be rapist townies blind and succeed at evacuating Lot and his family.

Postscript to Sodom and Gomorrah: As we all know, one of the angels tells Lot and his family not to look back as they are fleeing. Lot's wife disobeys and is turned into a pillar of salt. Question to my readers: Does anyone know why she is turned into a pillar of salt? Maybe salt was prevalent in the area, but, hey, so was sand. What's going on here? What exactly is the significance of "salt?" Why "salt"

and not some other seasoning or condiment? Was salt a favored
local seasoning? I'm kind of stuck on this question and wondering
if anybody knows. Does anyone think, for example, that if the story
were set in Mumbai, that she would have been turned into a pile
of curry? If God were destroying Tijuana, would she perhaps have
been turned into a hill of beans? If you know or think you do, tweet
me.

7

THE SACRIFICE OF ISAAC

So we know that God is crazy. He's capable of absolutely anything. He kicked Adam and Eve out of the Garden of Eden because they ate a piece of fruit that he told them not to eat. He made sure that everybody hated and feared the serpent and made him crawl on his belly because he talked Eve into eating the fruit. When he got fed up with the evil behavior of the human beings he himself had created, he killed off everybody and everything on the planet except for Noah, his family, and all those lucky pairs of animals and insects (at least the ones that weren't sacrificed the minute they got off the ark). He fucked over the city planners and architects of Babel because he thought they were getting too big for their breeches, dispersing them out to the farthest reaches of the planet all speaking different languages. He sealed his patriarchal deal with Abraham by telling him to make sure that he and every male member of his family and household cut off the tips of their dicks. He destroyed Sodom and Gomorrah and turned Lot's wife into, of all things, a pillar of salt.

So the lesson is that you really do not want to mess around with God because you just don't know what he's going to do—even if he likes you. I mean Abraham is clearly one of his all-time guys, definitely in the top ten, maybe even the top five of all time, although I admit that top lists are always subject to debate and controversy.

And yet, maybe because God liked Abraham so much, he decided for precisely that reason to fuck with him. He decided to test him. He wanted to test Abraham's blind loyalty. He wanted to find out if Abraham would do anything he told him to do, no matter how horrible it was, because he, God, was the one telling him to do it. And so he came up with the ultimate test, the ultimate jest. He told Abraham to take his beloved son, Isaac, with him on a trip and when he got to his destination to kill him as a "burnt offering."

Abraham is cool with this directive from God from the get-go. He doesn't hesitate for one second. He doesn't blink. He's right there ready to kill his son because God wants him to, and above all else he wants to please God.

Fortunately, an angel jumps in at the last second and saves the boy. And God rewards Abraham for his blind loyalty, telling him that he will have even more offspring than ever, more offspring than there are stars in the sky and grains of sand on the seashore.

But here is where we need to take a step back and ask if any of this really makes any sense. If you think that God is telling you to do something horrific, or if you think that there is some higher purpose served by doing something horrific, is it OK to do the horrific thing to serve that higher purpose? Kierkegaard famously framed this question in Fear and Trembling by asking if there could ever be a teleological suspension of the ethical. His answer was, "yes." If God tells you to kill your son, you should suspend your ethical obligation not to kill your son and go ahead and kill him to serve the higher purpose of obeying God's command. Kierkegaard thought that if God did not have the power to suspend his own ethical system, if God did not have the power to negate what was right and what was wrong, then he was not all powerful and was not truly God.

In taking this position, Kierkegaard opens the door to justifying every conceivable atrocity that has ever been perpetrated by the dictators, terrorists and psycho killers of this god-forsaken world—fanatics who always posit that there is some higher purpose to be served, whether that be an Aryan nation, a dictatorship of the proletariat or the re-establishment of the caliphate.

The right answer to the question of whether there can ever be a teleological suspension of the ethical is a resounding "no." And that is because what is ethical does not proceed from a directive established by an irrational and power crazy God but from the reciprocal relations existing naturally between human beings who share the same needs, wants and goals. Call it the Golden Rule. Or say as the Beatles did that "the love you make is equal to the love you take." For that way lies the path with heart. Take the other path, and you end up in Jonestown or North Korea.

Sorry. That might not be funny. But it surely is true.

8

BROTHERLY LOVE

One of the first lessons you learn from reading the Bible is that you can't trust anybody. Just think of what brothers do to one another. Cain kills his brother, Abel, after God likes Abel's gift better. As I said, fruit is the last thing you want to give God. It's just going to remind him of Adam and Eve, and you know something bad is bound to happen. But for Cain to turn on his brother, Abel, and kill him over this little slight from God is really shocking. It shows right from the beginning that you just can't count on anybody to be honorable and true—not even a member of your own family.

Consider the story of Isaac, Rebekah, Esau and Jacob. After surviving death at the hands of his own father, Isaac marries Rebekah. Like Sarah, Rebekah initially has a hard time conceiving a child. Finally God answers Isaac's prayers, and Rebekah is pregnant with twins. But something is wrong from the beginning. The twins do not seem to get along, even though they are still in the womb. Rebekah asks God what is going on. It turns out the sibling rivalry is his idea. He tells Rebekah that "two nations are in your womb, and two peoples from within you shall be divided; the one shall be stronger than the other, and the older shall serve the younger."

So here we go again. It turns out Isaac favors Esau, the older boy, the hairy hunter, while Rebekah prefers Jacob, the more con-

templative and quiet one, who dwells "in tents." Now I have to side
with Rebekah here because it's clear that Esau is not the brightest
guy on the block. One day Esau comes home hungry and exhausted
from a rough outing in the fields and wants some of Jacob's stew.
Jacob agrees to give him some but only if he exchanges the stew
for his birthright. Incredibly, Esau agrees. Yes, Esau sells his entire
inheritance to his brother, Jacob, for a bowl of stew. Then Esau has
the nerve to be touchy about it from then on, claiming that Jacob
cheated him.

The favoritism and bad blood between the brothers come to
a head when Isaac is old and blind and tells Esau he wants to give
him his blessing before he dies. Esau is supposed to go hunting and
prepare a meal for the old man from the game that he has killed
and then return with the meal for his blessing. Rebekah hears the
conversation and decides no way is that happening. Her favorite,
Jacob, has got to get the blessing instead. She tells Jacob to go out
and kill two goats so that she can make a delicious goat dinner for
Isaac. Apparently this is one of his favorite dishes. She prepares the
meal, has Jacob dress in Esau's clothes and then covers his arms in
the goatskins, thinking that Isaac will then be deceived into thinking that the smooth and cerebral Jacob is the hairy hunter Esau.
This seems preposterous, of course. How could anybody think that
goatskins were hairy arms? But it turns out that Rebekah knows
her man. Whether he's not as sharp as he used to be or whether he
carried the dumb gene and gave it to Esau, the ruse works. Isaac
mistakes Jacob for Esau even though he recognizes Jacob's voice,
and he gives his blessing to the younger son by mistake.

When Esau returns and discovers what has happened, he is devastated and asks his father to give him a blessing, too. But Isaac says, sorry I gave it already to Jacob; as if he had just one blessing to give and now it's gone. Esau insists, and then Isaac decides to give him a blessing after all—a bad one—telling him basically that he will have a hard life and have to serve his brother, although he will eventually break the yoke of his servitude. The episode ends with Esau vowing to kill Jacob and Jacob fleeing for his life.

Then there's the story of Jacob's twelve sons. Keeping up the tradition of favoritism, Jacob prefers Joseph, the youngest. Jacob broadcasts his favoritism of Joseph by giving him a coat of many colors. As you might expect, Joseph's brothers hate him. When Joseph shares with his brothers a couple of dreams that suggest that he will rule over them, they hate him even more. All of the brothers want to kill him except Reuben, who suggests they go easy on him and just throw him into a pit. He plans on rescuing Joseph when his brothers leave the scene. The brothers strip Joseph of his colorful coat and throw him into the pit. Reuben somehow leaves the scene, and when the remaining brothers see a group of traders approaching, they decide, why kill Joseph when they can make some money on him, and so they sell their brother into slavery, and he is taken away to Egypt.

The upshot of all of this intrigue is rather mixed and messy. Despite having been sold into slavery, Joseph becomes a big shot in Egypt, second only to the Pharaoh in power, because of his extraordinary ability to interpret dreams and his CEO-like management skills. We also learn from Joseph himself that God was the puppet master behind his brothers' treachery, so ultimately he doesn't blame them. He was actually sent by God to Egypt to be in position to save everybody from famine. When all is forgiven, Joseph invites his whole family to come down and live with him in Egypt. That's how all of the tribes of Israel end up there. When the Pharaoh, who is Joseph's champion, dies, the new Pharaoh turns on the people of Israel, and they are then all thrust into slavery for generations to come.

9

MOSES

You have to say that Moses was a pretty lucky guy. For some reason his mother didn't want anybody to know that he was around. When she couldn't hide him any longer, she stuck him in a basket and left him by a riverbank whereupon he is promptly found by none other than the Pharaoh's daughter. Now that's pretty lucky. Eventually Moses is adopted by the Pharaoh's daughter, and he lives a dual existence. He is a Hebrew, one of the oppressed people, and he is also a member of the Pharaoh's family, the Pharaoh who is enslaving the Hebrew people.

Moses comes out of the closet as a man of the people when he sees an Egyptian beating a fellow Hebrew. First he looks around to make sure nobody else is watching, and when he doesn't see anybody, he beats the Egyptian guy to death and buries him in the sand. The next day, however, Moses finds out that he was wrong. It turns out that word has gotten around about the killing, and when the Pharaoh finds out, he wants to kill Moses. So Moses takes off and stays in another town by the name of Midian, where he promptly helps out a priest's seven daughters. The girls are being hassled by a bunch of mean shepherds. Moses drives away the shepherds, and the father gives him one of his daughters to marry.

Next thing you know, the King of Egypt is dead. God suddenly remembers that his people are enslaved and that he hasn't really been living up to the circumcision deal that he made with Abraham way back when. God decides that Moses is the guy to help, and he appears to him from inside a burning bush.

No matter how many times I read this passage, I find myself disappointed. This is the God who kicked Adam and Eve out of the Garden of Eden with such chutzpah and aplomb. This is the God who drowned everybody and everything on earth except for Noah and his family and a few million animals and insects. This is the God who left the Tower of Babel builders dazed and confused when he scattered them across the far corners of the earth and whipped out all of those different languages, and here he decides to pull a cheap parlor trick when he first appears to Moses. It's as if Criss Angel were to show up at a kid's birthday party to do some clumsy card tricks.

Anyway Moses is very impressed with the Burning Bush, and to be fair, that's really all that counts. He's even more impressed when God tells him that he wants him to go back to Egypt and free the Israelites from their captivity. Moses is initially a little nervous about whether or not he is up to the task. He plans on telling everybody that God has sent him to be their liberator, but not surprisingly he wants to be able to provide a little more information just in case there are a few people who don't believe that he was sent to them by the creator of the universe. For example, he'd at least like to be able to tell them what God's name is—besides God, that is.

God tells Moses to say that he was sent by "I AM WHO I AM." When Moses hears this, he's still a little skeptical, and I think we can all sympathize. I AM WHO I AM sounds a little silly. If you'll forgive the anachronism, it reminds me a bit of Robin Williams, as Popeye the Sailor Man, singing, "I yam what I yam but I yam what I yam," etc.

To bolster Moses's confidence a little further, God, who's apparently still stuck in magic trick mode, teaches Moses how to turn a staff into a serpent and then back into a staff again; how to make his hand turn white as snow; and last but not least, how to turn water from the Nile into blood. Unfortunately Moses is still pretty nervous, insisting that he's not such a great talker. God starts getting a little impatient here and tells Moses again not to worry, that he will actually be doing all of the talking for Moses anyway, and with this last bit of assurance, Moses is finally ready to go out and save the Israelites from the Egyptians.

GOD AND MOSES LIBERATE THE PEOPLE OF ISRAEL

Now here's where God really gets his mojo back. Even though God is speaking for Moses, the Israelites don't pay any attention to him. So Moses knows that if he can't get his own people to believe him, he's not going to get anywhere with the Pharaoh. But God is already one step ahead of Moses.

God is planning on having a little fun. He tells Moses that initially he will "harden the Pharaoh's heart" so that he doesn't listen to Moses. This little ploy gives God a chance to really strut his stuff and show the Pharaoh exactly who's the boss. Now it's hard to know how long the Pharaoh would have held out if he had been left to his own devices, but with God pulling the puppet strings the Pharaoh remains incredibly stubborn and God gets to hit Egypt with a seemingly endless series of plagues. Just listing the plagues is pretty impressive:

Plague #1: God turns the Nile to blood.

Plague #2: Now there are frogs everywhere.

Plague #3: Would you like a plague of gnats?

Plague #4: Or how about millions of flies?

Plague #5: God kills all of Egypt's livestock—all the horses, camels, sheep and goats.

Plague #6: Everybody breaks out in terrible boils.

Plague #7: Now it's starting to hail, and hello, this is Egypt.

Plague #8: At this point God actually brags to Moses that he is stringing this whole thing out so he can show everybody how powerful he is and what a tremendous number of signs he's capable of. Now he hits Egypt with his famous plague of locusts, and the locusts eat everything that's not nailed down.

Plague #9: If that isn't enough, God puts on a total eclipse of the sun for three whole days.

Despite all this, God still hasn't had enough, and neither has the Pharaoh. God continues to harden the Pharaoh's heart so that he can display one last great demonstration of his power. In the true tradition of God, the mass murderer, for his final plague God goes out around midnight and kills the firstborn child of every Egyptian household. For good measure he even kills the firstborn of the cattle, too, although I thought that he had already taken care of them when he killed all of the livestock in Plague #5. Of course, he spares all of the Israelite families. He tells them to kill a lamb and smear its blood on their houses. He also gives them a recipe for roasted lamb. Of course, this was the night of the first Passover.

Finally God softens the Pharaoh's heart. The Pharaoh gives in, and the Israelites flee Egypt. But God is still not done showing the

Pharaoh who's in charge. After the Israelites have gotten away, God hardens the Pharaoh's heart again. The Pharaoh decides that he's made a big mistake letting the Israelites go. He gathers up his army and takes off after them. This gets the Israelites really scared, and they think that maybe they were better off staying slaves rather than dying at the hands of the Pharaoh's army way out in the wilderness.

Of course, God has the Israelites' backs. And he gives Moses the power to perform one of the greatest miracles of all time. He parts the Red Sea so that the Israelites can just walk on through. When the Egyptians pursue them through the opening in the sea, God empowers Moses to let the waters return, and the entire Egyptian army is wiped out.

11

THE TEN COMMANDMENTS

Now you would think that after God has freed the Jewish people from captivity that they would have some confidence in him and Moses. But, no. Right before God stepped in and parted the Red Sea, the Israelites were complaining that they were better off living as slaves in Egypt. Now as soon as food runs out, they panic, think they're about to starve, and right away wish they were back in Egypt. God steps in again and sends them bread clouds to rain down manna from heaven, and the food problem is solved. (Of course, the only downside to this is that they end up eating this bread every day for the next forty years.)

Of course, in the desert, you're bound to have problems with water. Sure enough, next thing you know, the people are out of water, and it's the same old story. It doesn't matter that God just fed them when they were hungry. Now they think they're going to die of thirst. God has Moses do a magic trick. Water comes flying out of a rock, and the whole thirst problem is solved.

So at this point you realize that, yes, God is crazy, but in fairness to him these people are a mess. He created them, so it's ultimately all his fault. That's the elephant in the room. It always was and always will be, but let's just set that aside for now. What's done is done. How do you make the best of a bad situation? Well, maybe if there are some clear-cut rules that will help.

So God comes up with the Ten Commandments.

Good idea? Might have been, but as they say, God is in the details. If you really want to be honest, the first four commandments wreck everything. They're all about God. He just can't get over himself.

1. You shall have no gods before me.

2. You shall not make a carved image.

3. You shall not take the name of your God in vain.

4. Remember the Sabbath day to keep it holy. The seventh day is a Sabbath to the Lord your God.

God sounds like a jealous lover here. OK, people, he says. If you want to have a relationship with me, if you want things to stay good around here, don't even think about another god. Don't even look at a picture of another god. Watch what you say about me because it'll get back to me, and one day a week don't even think of going anywhere or doing anything except worshipping me. That day is all about me. Actually every minute of every day—it's always and everywhere about me. And don't even think of cheating on me. If you do, you're dead.

Now to be fair, the rest of the commandments aren't bad for the most part. After getting out of the way the rather quaint notion that you should be nice to your father and mother, it's all Basic Instinct.

Don't kill.

Don't commit adultery

Don't steal.

Don't lie.

Don't covet.

Now the "don't kill" commandment might seem obvious, but what you realize as you read the Bible is that God is against you killing anybody because he reserves that right to himself. So we have quite a double standard here. On the other hand, if he tells you to kill somebody, even if it's your own son, or if he tells you to go into a town and slaughter everybody, including little boys and girls, you need to follow those orders unless and until he tells you otherwise.

One other point: The prohibition against "coveting" is especially good because it reminds everybody that God knows what you're thinking. He is the ultimate Thought Police. He knows what's in your mind, and he knows what's in your heart, so don't imagine for one second that you can get away with anything. In the Catholic Church of the 1950s and 60s, this concept morphed into the idea that you could not have an impure thought, i.e., a sexual thought. Well, you could, but you had to say to yourself, "Oh, my God! I'm having a sexual thought. I hate that. Out thought! Out!" If you liked the thought, if you liked that your dick was getting hard or your clit was stiffening, then you had just committed a mortal sin and were heading for hell. Just a thought, a single thought, and you would be tortured with fire and brimstone forever.

So those are the Ten Commandments. I will give God credit for one thing here. He does get the theatrics right. There's thunder, lightning, a cloud of smoke and a trumpet blast, and he has Moses go all the way up a mountain to get the commandments. Now this is all good stuff. No doubt about it. But right away everything goes off the rails as far as laws and commandments are concerned. God has a fit of law making. Talk about OCD. Once he starts making laws, he just can't stop. All of a sudden there are laws about everything: laws about owning slaves, laws about what to pay the father if you seduce a virgin, laws about what you can and can't eat, laws about having sex with animals (if you do it, you'll be executed), laws about bodily discharges, and on and on and on.

12

WEIRD LAWS

Here are some of the weird laws that God establishes:

Killing:

If you beat another person to death, you are put to death unless God helped you by letting the person you wanted to kill fall into your hands. If that's how you caught the guy you wanted to kill, then you are not put to death. Instead you are given a place to flee.

You have a moral obligation to kill a sorceress, i.e., a female witch.

If you catch somebody doing work on the Sabbath, you can kill him. It doesn't have to be much work. The guilty party could be mowing his lawn or doing laundry, and it would be OK to execute him. While the Israelites were wandering around the desert, they found a man gathering sticks on the Sabbath. When they brought him in, God told Moses that the guy should be taken outside the camp and everybody should gang up on him and stone him to death. And that's what they did.

Assault:

If you have an argument with some guy and you get mad and beat the crap out of him and the guy is able one day to walk again, then you are in the clear. You just have to pay the guy's medical bills and also pay him for lost time—sort of like a disability payment.

If you beat a pregnant woman to such an extent that she miscarries and dies, then you must die too, but if she delivers prematurely, lives and the child survives, you just pay a fine to the husband. I don't know what the rule is in this case if the husband gave the beating.

Law Concerning Witnesses:

If somebody commits a crime against you—let's say they rape you or assault you—and nobody else sees it and you're the only witness, you are out of luck. Your victimizer has committed the perfect crime because God has established that a single witness is insufficient "against a person for any crime for any wrong in connection with any offense that he has committed. Only on the evidence of two or of three shall a charge be established." Clearly one witness is not enough. But how many are enough? Is it two, or is it three witnesses? I'm not sure. Anyway you can apparently commit any crime you want so long as nobody else but the victim sees you.

Beyond the rules governing violent crimes, there are a whole lot of curious prohibitions and laws. Here are a few:

No tattoos. God does not like them. I don't know what he thinks about nipple piercing.

Men cannot wear women's clothing, and women cannot wear men's clothing. God considers cross-dressing an abomination.

If you find a bird's nest with the mother and chicks and maybe some eggs in it, you cannot grab them all. You have to leave the mother, but you can take the chicks and the eggs and eat them because that brings good luck.

Do not boil a young goat in its mother's milk—I don't know if this is primarily a prohibition against boiling or if it's really about the mother's milk. For example, maybe it's OK to boil the kid in water or in the milk of a goat that's not its mother. Also, I wonder if you barbecue the young goat, can you use its mother's milk as a tenderizer.

You cannot plow a field using an ox and a donkey together.

You cannot wear wool and linen clothing at the same time.

If you are walking in your neighbor's vineyard, you can eat as many of his grapes as you want, but you cannot take any home with you.

If you are in a camp and have a wet dream, you have to leave the camp, find some water to wash off and then wait until sunset to come back to the camp.

You cannot take a shit in the camp. You need to go out of the camp, dig a hole with a trowel, shit in the hole and then cover it all up. However, there is no instruction on wiping.

If you are living with your married brother and he dies without having a son and you refuse to marry his wife, then she can go up to you in the presence of the elders, pull off your sandal and spit in your face.

If you're fighting with another man and your wife tries to help you by coming up and grabbing him by the balls, she gets her hand cut off.

If you are blind, lame or have a fucked up face; if one arm or leg is longer than the other; if you have any hand or foot injury; if you are a hunchback or a dwarf; if you have itchy, dry skin; if you somehow got your testicles crushed or your dick cut off—however that happened—you cannot approach the altar and make an offering to God. It doesn't matter how religious or devoted you are, stay away. You are too fucked up and disgusting to get close to God.

13

WHAT GETS YOU THE DEATH PENALTY

There is an amazing list of things that will get you the death penalty. I've already mentioned a few like beating somebody to death or doing your laundry on the Sabbath. Here are some more:

- Hitting your father or mother.

- Cursing your father or mother.

- Cursing or blaspheming God.

- Worshipping any other god.

- Sacrificing your child to another god.

- Stealing a man and selling him—both the kidnapper and the buyer must die.

- A man having sex with another man—both of them must die.

- Being a prostitute if your father is a priest; if your father is not a priest, you get to keep on living.

- Having a three-way with a woman and her mother—that gets all three of you burned to death.

- Fucking another man's wife—you and the wife both die.

- Fucking a betrothed virgin in the city—you and the virgin both die unless she cries out for help, since the assumption is that in the city someone would hear her cries.

- Fucking a betrothed virgin in the country—just you die since the assumption is that even if the virgin cried out, no one would hear her.

- Fucking an animal—the animal gets killed too whether it stood still or not.

- Mistreating a widow or fatherless child—apparently if you mistreat a married woman or a child who has a father, you may be punished, but you still get to live.

- Being a "stubborn and rebellious son" —if your father and mother get really frustrated with you, they can turn you in to the elders of the city and have you stoned to death.

- Pretending to be a virgin—if you get married and your husband thinks you're a virgin and you're not and he hates you for whatever reason, he can have you stoned to death.

- If you claim to be able to communicate with the dead, if you are a medium or a necromancer, guess what? You get to join the dead—John Edward, look out!

- If you are a false prophet speaking on behalf of false gods

- If you refuse to follow the legal decision of a priest or a judge

• If you accuse someone of a capital crime and you are lying and you are found out, then you die, for "it shall be life for life, eye for eye, tooth for tooth, hand for hand, foot for foot."

• If you were so unlucky as to be born an Amorite, a Girgashite, a Hittite, a Perizzite, a Canaanite, a Hivite or a Jebusite. If you were born into one of these communities, you are dead. God has promised your land and your home to the people of Israel, so you and your entire family, friends and neighbors must die. Even the babies must go. Sorry.

14

What Is OK

So a lot of the laws and punishments are pretty strange, but what is absolutely shocking is what's actually OK to do. Here is a list of things that are perfectly fine to do, as far as God is concerned:

- Own slaves.

- Sell your daughter into slavery.

- Beat your slave with a stick as long as he survives for a day or two after the beating. If the slave dies right away, however, you're in trouble.

- Seduce a virgin so long as you pay her father and marry her, and if for some reason the father won't let you marry his daughter after you raped her, you're still OK if you pay him the right amount of money.

- Have sex with another man's slave as long as you sacrifice a ram afterwards.

- Marry a female captive after you have shaved her head, cut her nails and given her a month to mourn the death of her parents, whom you've killed.

- If you threaten to attack a faraway city and the people of that city surrender, then you should just enslave all of the inhabitants and not kill anybody. However, if they actually have the nerve to defend themselves, then when you defeat them, you should kill every adult male. You then own all of the women, children and livestock, and you can do whatever you want with them.

- In cases in which God says that you should take over another city as your rightful inheritance, you should slaughter everyone—all of the men, women and children have to die.

- However, when you attack a city, particularly if the siege takes a long time, be sure that you don't destroy any of the fruit trees.

15

WHAT YOU CAN EAT AND WHAT YOU CAN'T EAT

There are also a whole bunch of laws about what you can and can't eat.

You can eat cows, but you can't eat camels, rabbits or pigs.

Fish are fine to eat, but shellfish are not.

Lots of birds are on the "don't eat" list. Examples include eagles, vultures, falcons, sea gulls, hawks and owls.

I'm not sure who would want to, but don't eat bats. God thinks they're birds. They're actually mammals, but the point is—don't eat them.

Don't eat any winged insects except for locusts, crickets and grasshoppers.

Rats and lizards are out. The GEICO gecko is also safe. Don't eat it.

Blood. Don't eat blood. I guess that means no steaks rare or medium rare.

Finally, fruit. God really has a thing about fruit. If you buy a new property and grow fruit trees on it, you cannot eat the fruit for the first three years. Actually in the fourth year you have to offer the fruit to God, so you can't eat it then either. In the fifth year it's OK to eat the fruit.

16

THE GOLDEN CALF

Now let's get back to the story of Moses and the people of Israel in the desert, and this part is rather strange. Moses has apparently been spending too much time up on Mount Sinai hanging out with God, and the people of Israel are tired of waiting for him to come back. They're fed up with God, too, and they want to replace him with an idol—this despite all that God and Moses have done for them. They go to Aaron, Moses's brother, with their complaint and unaccountably he agrees right away to accommodate them—once again you just can't trust your brother.

Aaron has the people gather up all of their jewelry, and he somehow turns it all into a golden calf. Immediately, in an act that defies all logic, the people begin worshipping the golden calf (formerly their necklaces and earrings) as the god that led them out of Egypt. Now not surprisingly God finds out about the betrayal right away and wants to hit his Chosen People with some sort of disaster that will kill off most of them in retribution. Moses persuades God not to kill everybody by telling him that the Egyptians will gossip about him and spread the story that he led the people of Israel out of Egypt just so he could kill them all off in the desert. But when Moses confronts the people about what they've done, he gets so angry that he breaks the tablets that contain the Ten Commandments and destroys the golden calf. Then he orders the loyal sons of

Levi to kill their own brothers, friends and neighbors to prove their loyalty to God. Next thing you know, God whips a plague on the people to get them back for what they've done despite having told Moses that he would let the people slide. After God cools off a bit, he decides that the Israelites will still be his Chosen People and that he will drive numerous people off their land to make it happen. He also demonstrates uncharacteristic restraint by deciding to keep a distance from the Israelites, saying "I will not go up among you lest I consume you on the way."

17

FORTY YEARS IN THE DESERT

We know that the people of Israel have a tendency to complain and not trust God. Well, they complained just one time too many. God makes a wonderful promise to the Israelites. Basically he tells them that he'll let them go in and kill or enslave everybody in Canaan and take over their land because Canaan would be a great place for the Israelites to live. Nice.

God tells Moses to send out a spying party to check out Canaan. So they spy on Canaan for forty days. When they come back, they say, yeah, Canaan is great. It's the land of milk and honey, but there's just one problem. The people who live there are big and strong and they won't just let us take away their land. In fact, they'll defeat us and a lot of us will get killed.

God is furious at the spies' lack of faith. He wants to whip a plague on the Israelites and kill them all. Moses tries to calm God down and again tells him that if he wipes out the people of Israel, the Egyptians will gossip about him and say that he killed them because he wasn't powerful enough to bring them into Canaan.

This argument works, and so instead of wiping out the people of Israel, he sentences them to wander in the desert. They get one year for every day the spying party was out—a total of forty years. It's as if God builds a big invisible electric fence out in the desert, and the Israelites have to stay inside. They can't get out of the desert no matter how hard they try even though you would think that they could have pretty easily just walked from Egypt to Canaan in under a month since it's a distance of only 250 miles.

Interesting factoid: If you walked ten miles a day every day for forty years, you would travel 146,000 miles. That's the equivalent of traveling around the circumference of the earth almost six times.

Postscript to Forty Years in the Desert: God makes Moses take the fall for the Chosen People's lack of faith here as well. He tells Moses that no one from his generation, including him, will see the Promised Land. They will all die in the desert, never reaching that epic goal.

18

PEOPLE TO MOSES: WHAT HAVE YOU DONE FOR ME LATELY?

So Moses saves the people from total destruction at the hands of God, and what thanks does he get in return? A rebellion. Two hundred fifty chiefs led by a guy named Korah confront Moses and Aaron and basically say what's so special about you? Hey, who made you the holy one?

Now I'm sure Moses was laughing to himself at this affront, thinking, "That would be God, asshole."

Moses tells the rebels to assemble the next morning before God and that God will decide who is holy. I'll bet he couldn't wait until morning. God shows up and tells Moses and Aaron to stand back. He's ready to kill everybody whether they were part of the rebellion or not. Moses intercedes again for the rest of the people and God relents. Moses tells everybody else to steer clear of the bad guys. Then God orchestrates one of his most impressive and dramatic mass killings. He makes the ground open up, and he swallows up all of the bad guys—but in typical God fashion it's not just the bad guys. It's their wives and children and all of their possessions too. Everybody gets buried alive and goes to Sheol, which was just kind of a big mass grave.

It seems that heaven and hell weren't around then. Maybe they were, but they weren't open for business, or maybe God hadn't invented them yet. Who knows? I'll talk more about heaven and hell later. All I'll say right now is I wonder what happened to all of the people who were sent to Sheol when God came up with heaven and hell. Did they stay in Sheol, or were they promoted or demoted, with the good people going to heaven and the bad people going to hell?

It could not have been easy, especially if you are claustrophobic or scared of the dark, to be sent down to spend eternity in a cold, dark mass grave with maybe thousands or even millions of other people all crowded together with you. Even if everybody is a shade or a spirit or whatever you want to call not having a body, you really wouldn't have any privacy with everybody piled up together. So I would think that if you got promoted to heaven, whatever heaven is, you'd be pretty happy. But suppose you were a bad guy, and all of a sudden you were in hell. That would have to be a shock. Maybe after hundreds of years you had actually sort of gotten used to Sheol a little bit, and you're thinking, OK, maybe I can handle this. Then one day things are very different. Maybe suddenly you're in a totally different place, or maybe God just remodeled Sheol and moved in a lot of heating equipment. Anyway the temperature has just gone crazy—it's like a million or even a billion degrees, and you are burnt to a crisp—except that the fire never goes out. Now that shows more than anything else that I can think of that you should never think that things are so bad that they can't get any worse. At least not until you find yourself in hell, and then that's as bad as it can possibly get.

19

GOD'S WAR CRIMES

Don't mess with God. Don't do it. If he catches you doing bad stuff like fucking the livestock or worshipping anybody else but him, you're as good as dead. And if he doesn't get you now, don't worry, he'll get you later just when you think you're safe—that is when you're already dead, and you think, OK. I'm dead. That's it. No. You're wrong. The bad times are just beginning because that's when God steps in and sends you to Sheol, that big dark grave, or hell, which is sort of like a gigantic pizza oven, and you can never get out no matter how much you want to or how hard you try and you just have to stay there and suffer constantly unimaginable torments forever and ever without end.

Now let's say you're a three-year-old little boy living in a place called Midian and you're too young to have fucked a goat and you've never heard of God and you don't even know who the other gods are. Would you be in the clear? The answer is no. Now you might have had a really miserable life anyway since you had the bad luck to be born more than three thousand years ago in the middle of a fucking desert without indoor plumbing or toilet paper or schools or books of any kind, so you were pretty much doomed to walk around stinking and illiterate for the entirety of your pitiful life. But you wouldn't have known any better and what surely would stink to us would probably be just fine with you. No matter. You never get the chance to live the high life.

You see you were born in the wrong town and were living with the wrong people. No two ways about it. It boils down to that and nothing else. You were simply born in the wrong place at the wrong time.

God has promised the people of Israel that they can live in a particular area that is really nice. It's the land of "milk and honey." It's far and away the best place to live in the entire desert. Only one problem. People already live there.

Guess what? That's not a problem to God. As I mentioned previously, all of those people—the Amorites, Girgashites, Hittites, Perizzites, Canaanites, Hivites and Jebusites—get the death penalty. They all get completely wiped out, wiped off of the face of the earth, not a single person survives, courtesy of God, Himself.

Now one might think that a little Midianite boy would be safe. After all he is not one of the people who have been marked for death. In fact, Moses's father-in-law, Jethro, was a Midianite priest, and Moses lived in Midian for years when he was hiding from the Pharaoh. So Midian should be safe. But no! By the time the Israelites are in the neighborhood of Midian, God has empowered them to begin wiping out anybody who is in their way. They've already gotten to the Amorites and have taken over all of their land. Now the people of Moab, another kingdom in the neighborhood, know what's been going on, and they are, not surprisingly, scared

to death. They reach out to the people of Midian and establish an
alliance to defend themselves. Now remember if God wants to
take over your town, you have no right to defend yourself, so this
only makes things worse for the Moabites and also the Midianites.
What's more, they hire a guy, actually an oracle, named Balaam
to curse God. But God is right on top of the situation. He goes to
Balaam and gives him the lowdown on the Chosen People and tells
him to give a blessing rather than a curse. So the fix is in.

To make matters worse, the people of Israel begin mingling
with the people of Moab. They worship Baal, the Moab god, and
they fuck around with the Moab women. Very bad idea. God finds
out and has Moses hang all of the chiefs of the people of Israel.
He also whips a plague on the Israelites, which ends up killing
thousands of people. Then right as all of this is going on, another
Israelite guy brings a Midianite woman into his family. Apparently
he was taking her for a wife. Bad, bad, bad. Phineas, one of Aaron's
sons, finds out, and he goes right after the man and the woman and
stabs them both to death with a spear. God greatly approves of this
because once the man and the woman are speared, he stops the
plague, and he rewards Phineas by giving him and his descendants
a perpetual priesthood.

So now the Midianites are doomed. God tells Moses to go in
and wipe them out. And that's what Moses and his men do—well
sort of. At first they just kill every adult male and take possession of
the women, children and livestock. But when Moses finds out that
this is all they've done, he is furious. He apparently knows that this

was not what God had in mind. He wants to know why the commanders of his army let all of the women live. He orders them to
kill every woman who has had sex and to kill every male child as
well. So that's the end of our poor little three-year-old boy. Sorry
kid.

Moses does tell his commanders to let all of the female virgins
live. These would basically be little girls under the age of eleven or
twelve. He tells his guys they can keep them alive for themselves. I
guess that's what you call "booty."

Then in an amazing epilogue to the slaughter, God steps in and
tells Moses that when they divide up the plunder, which includes
the virgin girls and the livestock, that a portion needs to be set
aside for him as a tribute. I think this means that he wants a sacrifice in tribute to him. To be precise, for this tribute from the spoils
taken by the army, God gets 675 sheep, 72 cattle, 61 donkeys and
32 people. From plunder given to the people, God gets one of every
50 or ten times as much, and so he gets 6,750 sheep, 720 cattle, 610
donkeys and 320 people. I love the equivalence that we have here
between livestock and people. That just about says it all.

So that's the story of Midian, boys and girls. He kills all of the
people with the exception of prepubescent girls, and he lets most of
the livestock live. It's a good example of God's war crimes, of God's
acts of genocide. However, with respect to anybody actually living
in the Promised Land—once again, that would be the Amorites,
Girgashites, Hittites, Perizzites, Canaanites, Hivites and Jebusites—
nobody is allowed to live, not even the poor little girls. The only

way you live is if you are the odd exception, like Rahab, a prostitute who hides the Israelites who spy on Jericho immediately before the city is attacked and totally destroyed by fire. She and her family are spared as a reward for having betrayed their own people, but otherwise every man, woman and child is slaughtered, along with all of the oxen, sheep and donkeys.

As Moses says to the people of Israel, "In the cities of these peoples that the Lord your God is giving you for an inheritance, you shall save alive nothing that breathes, but you shall devote them to complete destruction." Oddly, this is where Moses expresses God's concern for the fruit trees. "When you besiege a city for a long time, making war against it in order to take it, you shall not destroy its trees by wielding an axe against them. You may eat from them, but you may not cut them down. Are the trees in the field human, that they may be besieged by you?" So Moses (speaking for God) states that it is perfectly fine to slaughter every single man, woman and child in a town that you are invading, but it is wrong to cut down a fruit tree.

Fruit—it's one of the weirdest motifs in the Old Testament.

20

LIFE IN THE PROMISED LAND

You would think that the repeated God-sponsored genocidal slaughtering of the people occupying the Promised Land would be enough to convince the people of Israel that they should stick with God and always be true to his laws. But no way. Once God clears out most of the natives and the Hebrew people take over the Promised Land, they stray from fidelity to God. It's basically that old irresistible urge to worship other gods. Sort of like the unquenchable lust for strange pussy. It's as if the Chosen People were serial adulterers and just couldn't stop themselves from cheating on God. Inevitably, when they do cheat, God punishes them and allows their enemies to defeat them and rule over them. Of course, these enemies are actually the people that God has been targeting for slaughter to make room for the Chosen People in the Promised Land. Now he decides to keep a goodly number of them around just so they can defeat and subjugate the people of Israel. Then, after awhile, he takes pity on the Hebrew people and sends in a special person called a judge to liberate them from subservience and captivity. But as soon as the judge dies, they go back to their evil ways. This vicious cycle goes on seemingly forever or at least for a few hundred years.

Now the Book of Judges is where we also come upon a royal fuckup in the continuity of the Bible. As we know, the people of Israel totally wiped out the Midianites except for the little virgin girls.

Everybody, except those little girls, was murdered. Moses working on behalf of God saw to that. Now somehow magically the Midianite people are back and have taken control over the people of Israel and are oppressing them. Sorry. That makes no sense.

Just so there's no confusion. Here's the order that a furious Moses gave to his commanders after they had screwed up and had limited themselves to killing all of the adult males in Midian: "Kill every male among the little ones, and kill every woman who has known man by lying with him. But all the young girls who have not known man by lying with him keep alive for yourselves."

So there was no one left in Midian but those poor little girls. And now in Judges the Midianites are magically back in full force oppressing the people of Israel who killed just about all of them back in Numbers. When I say "full force," I mean it. Somehow there are now so many Midianites you can't even count them. Here's how they are described: "Whenever the Israelites planted crops, the Midianites and the Amalekites and the people of the East would come up against them. They would encamp against them and devour the produce of the land, as far as Gaza, and leave no sustenance in Israel and no sheep or ox or donkey. For they would come up with their livestock and their tents; they would come like locusts in number—both they and their camels could not be counted—so that they laid waste to the land as they came in."

No use in rationalizing it. That's a fuck up. The stories just don't track. But, hey, what's the big deal? Nothing's perfect, including the Bible.

21

GOD AND GIDEON DEFEAT THE MIDIANITE ZOMBIES

Since there is no explaining how there are so many Midianites left to subjugate the people of Israel after the people of Israel killed them all, let's just think of them as the Midianite zombies. Here the story gets good because God once again cannot resist the urge to show off. It reminds me of when he wouldn't let the Pharaoh give in and allow the Chosen People to get the hell out of Egypt because he wanted to display his wondrous ability to whip up plagues.

Now he wants to defeat the Midianite zombies, but he does not want the Hebrew people to take any credit. He recruits a guy named Gideon to do it, and Gideon organizes an army of thousands of people, but God keeps telling him that his army is way too big. When Gideon finally whittles it down to just 300 people, he's finally satisfied. God's method of routing the Midianite zombies and their friends, "the Amalekites and the people of the East," shows his love of the theatrical. He has Gideon hand out trumpets, yes trumpets, to all 300 guys. How they came up with 300 trumpets, I have no idea. They also all get an empty jar and a torch. At this point it looks as though God and Gideon are ready to lead a team building exercise.

When Gideon begins blowing his trumpet, everybody blows theirs too and breaks their jars. Now they all have a torch in one hand and absurdly a trumpet in the other hand, and they're all shouting, "A sword for the Lord and for Gideon!" Somehow the cheerleading and the trumpet blowing scare the fearsome Midianite zombies and their pals, and they either run away or actually start killing one another.

I don't know what the total body count was, but we're told that 120,000 of the generically denominated "people of the East," met their end. None of this makes any sense, but I'm sure God was very pleased because nobody among the Hebrew people could possibly think that they had engineered such a preposterous routing and defeat of the Midianite zombies and their friends. There could not possibly be any other explanation for the extraordinary massacre aside from divine intervention.

22

THE WORST BROTHER OF ALL

One thing for sure, Gideon must have been a very busy guy. He not only defeated the Midianite zombies and then ruled over the people of Israel for forty years, he also had seventy sons with his many wives. There's no mention of how many daughters. I guess they don't count. In addition to the official sons, however, he also had a bastard son with his concubine, and that, as it turns out was a big mistake.

The bastard son's name is Abimelech, and he is a good candidate for the worst brother of all time. When his father dies, he goes to his relatives and asks, would you rather have all seventy sons rule over you, or me? Now this makes absolutely no sense, but all of the relatives agree that they'd prefer to be ruled over by Abimelech, and they pay him to take care of the situation.

Abimelech hires a bunch of thugs, and they go over together to Gideon's house, where conveniently all seventy of the brothers are gathered and execute all of them, we are told, "on one stone," except for the youngest, who somehow hides somewhere and escapes death. So much for honoring the memory of the great Gideon who liberated the people from the Midianite zombies and ruled for forty years. In fact, we learn that as soon as the executions are carried out, the people all get together and make Abimelech king.

23

DON'T MAKE A DEAL WITH GOD

What can I say? It is just so repetitive and boring, but it is what it is. The Chosen People worship other gods and are punished by God for their infidelity through subjugation to another people. Then God identifies a liberator, known as a judge, who defeats the oppressor, and the people of Israel are saved. Then they go off again worshipping some other god, and the cycle repeats. It really is just like serial infidelity or alcoholism or drug addiction. It's as if the people of Israel were in need of some heavy-duty rehab.

Now amid all of this repetitive action, we do get one story with an especially important lesson. It's the story of "Jephthah's Tragic Vow." At this point, the Israelites have really gone off the deep end in their cheating on God. They don't just worship one false god. They go on a rampage of idolatry and are promiscuously worshiping virtually every other god around, including "the Baals and the Ashtaroth, the gods of Syria, the gods of Sidon, the gods of Moab, the gods of the Ammonites, and the gods of the Philistines." Wow! I have no idea how they even had the time to worship all of those gods. Anyway God gets them back for this by allowing the Ammonites and the Philistines to rule over and oppress the people of Israel for eighteen years.

At this point a mighty warrior judge named Jephthah rises up among the Hebrew people, and he is intent on defeating the Am-

monites. He decides to make a deal with God. He tells God that he
will sacrifice to him whichever person happens to come out of his
home first to greet him after he defeats the Ammonites. Now this
is about as reckless and crazy as you can get, but apparently God is
totally fine with the deal. He enables Jephthah to defeat the Ammonites. When Jephthah returns home, his daughter is the first one
to greet him, so he is bound to kill her in keeping with the deal he's
made with God.

It's amazing how this story reads precisely like all of those other
stories about making a deal with the devil. In this case, after making a deal with God, Jephthah is enabled to accomplish a great
feat, namely the defeat of the Ammonites and the liberation of the
Hebrew people, but he must sacrifice his daughter to God to accomplish the task.

Oddly, we never even know the name of Jephthah's daughter.
All we know is that she is a virgin and that incredibly she is fine
with being killed because she understands that her father must
honor his deal with God. She simply asks for a two-month reprieve
so that she can go up to the mountains and weep for her virginity.
Jephthah grants her the two months of weeping, and when the two
months are up, he kills her.

24

SAMSON

There is one other incredible story among the repetition of idolatry and punishment in the Book of Judges, and that's the story of Samson, the very first superhero. Samson is blessed by God with extraordinary strength and is destined to save Israel from the Philistines. He first displays his amazing strength when, of all things, he encounters a lion, and he tears the lion apart with his bare hands. Later he kills thirty Philistine men all by himself and then sets fire to their grain stores and their olive orchards.

Interestingly, an army of 3,000 of his own people pursue Samson after the Philistines attack them in retaliation for Samson's actions. They tie him up and turn him over to the Philistines, but he breaks free of his bonds and kills 1,000 Philistines using the jawbone of a donkey as his only weapon. He goes on after this amazing feat to serve as a judge of the Israelites for twenty years. But the story does not end there. The Philistines are still out to get him. They believe that there is a secret to his incredible strength, and they bribe Samson's lover, Delilah, to find it out.

It's obvious that Samson has it really bad for Delilah. He plays along with her seduction game as she tries to get him to reveal his secret. Three times he gives her false answers. Then inexplicably he tells her—it's his hair. So a bald head is Samson's Kryptonite.

Delilah has a guy come and shave Samson's head while he's sleeping in her lap. Now that's a heavy sleeper. Once Samson's bald, the Philistines grab him and promptly gouge out his eyes. They keep him in prison rather than killing him so that they can humiliate him and exult in their victory over their great nemesis. They attribute their success to their god Dagon, which must have really irritated God, so you know that he will make sure to get them all.

Ridiculously, no one thinks of the obvious—that hair grows back—and nobody notices that Samson is no longer bald. While he's on display at a big party, the unshorn Samson pushes against two pillars that are holding up the entire building and kills all of the lords and ladies of the Philistines and himself as well.

25

PARTS YOU CAN SKIP

One of the good things about reading the Bible is that you can skip some of it. Life is short, so if you're busy or old or just have better things to do like day trading or organizing your closet, you can definitely skip parts of the Bible and not miss much. I mentioned how repetitive and dreary the action gets in Judges, so skip it except for the good parts. But Judges is hardly the worst book or section of the Bible. There are actually a lot of even more boring and useless sections. Here is a quick list of parts you can definitely skip:

• God's excruciatingly detailed instructions on the design of the Ark of the Covenant, the tabernacle, the altar, etc. I know the Ark of the Covenant and related stuff is important, but this is just too much information—the first time through. But then it's repeated later in Exodus.

• The laws about how to sacrifice animals in Leviticus. None of the information seems to be very useful to a reader in midtown Manhattan. However, I will say that just as you're about to give up on the entire book of Leviticus, your patience is repaid with a really good story. God gives the priests very precise instructions on how to kill the animals to please him—what to do with the blood and their various body parts and how to conduct the ceremony. When Nadab and Abihu, two sons of Aaron, screw up and light an unauthorized fire, God sends a fire to consume them. Zap! Just like that, they're dead. Next thing you know, Eleazar and Ithamar, Aaron's two remaining sons screw up, too. They burn up a goat offering, and Moses is really angry. You think for a second that Moses will pick up where God left off and kill them too, but Aaron, who seems to be Teflon, steps in and speaks up for them, saying he's made mistakes too in the past, and Moses backs off.

• A bunch of other laws: laws about grain offerings, purification after childbirth, leprosy, bodily discharges, and eating blood.

• Any passages having to do with a census, genealogies or lists of names—they're like reading old phone books.

• The arrangement of the people of Israel's camp.

• The list of everybody's offerings on the day the tabernacle was consecrated.

• All of the different offerings for all of the different occasions and feasts.

• All of the passages concerning the allotment of the Promised Land in the Book of Joshua—they're like reading records in the town clerk's office.

• Most of the songs. I don't know what their melodies were, but the lyrics are terrible.

• All of the sections of Deuteronomy, 1 Chronicles and 2 Chronicles that repeat stuff from previous Books. They say the Bible is perfect, but it appears that God needs an editor.

• The Minor Prophets. They're minor.

26

ANSWERED PRAYERS

Israel wants a king. God doesn't like it. He's the king they should be serving, and they are always unfaithful to him.

Samuel, the last of the judges, doesn't like the king idea either (actually he had appointed his sons as judges, but they turn out to be deadbeats, so they don't count). Samuel takes the people's clamoring for a king as a personal affront. But God says, don't take it that way. It's me they're rejecting, not you. Go back and tell them they can have a king, but let them know all of the problems of kings—how they'll exploit you and your children and all that you have. Just so you know, when they have a king, and they suffer under his rule and complain to me, I won't listen.

And that's what they call, "answered prayers."

So Israel gets its first king—Saul, anointed by Samuel. We're told that Saul stands out among all of the men of Israel because he's the handsomest and the tallest. However, these extraordinary regal qualifications do not prevent him from running afoul of God rather quickly.

Initially Saul does a tremendous job defeating all of Israel's enemies. He wipes out the Moabites, the Amorites, the Edomites, the kings of Zobah and the Philistines. However, when God tells him to attack the Amalekites and to kill every man, woman and child, including infants, as well as all of the livestock, he screws up. Now in fairness to Saul, he does pretty much kill every man, woman and child, including all of the infants. The one exception is that he captures rather than kills Agag, the Amalekite king. He also spares the best of the livestock— "the best of the sheep and of the oxen and of the fattened calves and the lambs." So once again, we see an interesting pattern—people are slaughtered, but livestock live because they have value as the spoils of war.

God tells Samuel that Saul has disobeyed his command by not killing absolutely everybody, including the king, and by keeping the best of the livestock. Samuel confronts Saul on God's behalf. He gives him a real tongue-lashing and fires him as king. Afterwards, the people still refer to him as king, but in actuality he is done.

After he fires Saul, Samuel has him produce, King Agag. The king thinks everything is cool and comes to Samuel with a big smile on his face. However, Samuel is in no mood to exchange pleasantries. As soon as he sees the king, he hacks him to pieces.

So Saul is out, and Israel is now without a king who enjoys God's favor, but God has his eye on a replacement—a rather unlikely replacement—a young boy, named David. At the same time, we are told that Saul is very depressed at having been discarded as king. He is desperately in need of cheering up. And who does he find to lift his spirits? None other than David, his soon-to-be-revealed successor. David is hired to play the lyre to bring a smile to the face of the pathetic erstwhile king. Clearly at this point Saul just can't catch a break. You have to hand it to God, the puppet master. He really knows how to rub it in.

27

DAVID AND GOLIATH

And now we come to one of the most famous stories of the Bible, David and Goliath. Unfortunately, it turns out that the whole thing is really just totally phony from beginning to end. The big death match between David, the weak and helpless, little, lyre-playing boy, and Goliath, the ten-foot tall, body-armored behemoth, has all of the authenticity of a WWE Championship match on pay-per-view.

To the uninformed observer, it would indeed appear that David has no chance whatsoever and that he is doomed to die in a suicidal attempt to defeat the invincible Philistine giant. The entire army of Israel is quaking with terror, but David knows that he has God on his side and that he can't be defeated. It seems that the people of Israel just never learn.

David dispatches Goliath with a single stone from his slingshot—bang! Straight to the head. He could have just as easily said, "Boo!" The big guy would have collapsed on the spot. Just to put an exclamation point on the whole thing, David cuts off Goliath's head and brings it back with him to Jerusalem. Unfortunately now that David is the people's hero, Saul hates the very sight of him. That's the end of the lyre playing. Saul turns into a raving lunatic. He even tosses his spear at David a couple of times, hoping to pin him to the wall, but David jumps out of the way.

28

FORESKINS

Now we are painfully aware of the fact that the people of Israel have a big fixation on circumcised penises. It's not really their fault. As we know, God decided that the way to seal his deal with them was for every guy to get the tip of his dick cut off. So far as I know, he never explained why, so I have no idea what he was thinking, although I'm pretty sure it wasn't to cut down on the incidence of STDs.

However, what we may not have known until we get to the story of David and Saul is that there was a whole different purpose to the cutting of foreskins as well. Apparently if you came back home with a freshly cut foreskin in your hand, presenting it, one imagines, in the manner of a proud little terrier dropping a dead mouse on its master's doorstep, you were greeted as a great conquering hero because it proved that you had killed one of the uncircumcised enemies of Israel.

With the failure of his attempts to kill the nimble David by spearing him against the wall, Saul decides that the best way to dispose of the boy is to have him die in battle. Why he thinks this will happen given David's legendary performance against Goliath, I have no idea. Anyway he tells David that he can marry his daughter, Michal, even though she is already betrothed to another guy and that he doesn't need to give him any money for his daughter. But he does want something instead—that would be 100 Philistine foreskins. Now that is a strange request. But David has absolutely no problem with it. He runs right out like somebody going to the grocery store to pick up a quart of milk and a dozen eggs and—surprise and delight—promptly returns with not 100, but 200, foreskins.

29

SAUL, THE HOMICIDAL MANIAC

It's important to point out that there is indeed a hidden hand behind both Saul's depression and his obsession with killing David. When Samuel fires Saul, we are told that "the Spirit of the Lord departed from Saul, and a harmful spirit from the Lord tormented him." After David kills Goliath, Saul is furious, and we learn that "a harmful spirit rushed upon Saul, and he raved within his house while David was playing the lyre." In fact, one of the ridiculous spear-chucking incidents is provoked by "a harmful spirit from the Lord." Once again, God is the ultimate mischief-maker. He just can't help himself, and so neither can Saul. He chases David all over the place, trying to kill him. When he finds out that a priest helped out David, he summons the offending priest along with all of his priestly colleagues and kills them all. Then in typical fashion he sends out his army to kill all of the people and livestock in the priests' hometown— "both man and woman, child and infant, ox, donkey and sheep."

There are lots of weird twists and turns to the story—e.g., David spares Saul's life twice because he won't kill one who has been anointed by God, but Saul still keeps trying to kill him anyway, and David winds up at one point actually living with his old nemesis, the Philistines. Indeed, it's only when Saul dies in a battle against the Philistines that his God-inspired homicidal mania against David finally comes to an end.

30

GOD'S FAVOR

God greatly favors David. The preeminent sign of his favor is that he enables David to defeat just about every other people within striking distance. He massacres their armies and he seizes their wealth. The list of the vanquished includes the Philistines, the Moabites, the king of Zobah, the Syrians, the Edomites and the Ammonites. Here are some highlights:

- He forces the Moabites to lie on the ground in three different lines; everybody in two of the lines is slaughtered; everybody in the remaining line is placed in servitude.

- The Syrians: two separate battles—in one, 20,000 killed; in the other, "the men of 700 chariots and 40,000 horsemen" are killed.

- The Edomites: 18,000 killed.

It's good to be king, especially when you are favored by God. But for everybody else in the neighborhood, all I can say is "Look out!"

31

KILLING: WHEN IS IT OK? WHEN IS IT NOT OK?

Here is a clear moral lesson, a clear differentiation between when killing is just fine and when it's not:

All of the mass slaughter of war when God is on your side is OK. It doesn't matter how many people you kill. In fact, quite often God wants you to kill everybody—every man, woman and child, including infants. While you're at it, kill all of the livestock, too. For that is God's will. However, making sure one particular guy dies— that would be a guy named Uriah—when you, David, want to steal his wife, Bathsheba, has nothing to do with God's will. That has to do with you getting your rocks off, so that kind of killing is bad.

Now that is about as clear a moral lesson as I can think of, and if you stick to the first kind of killing and never do the second, you are sure to stay on the good side of God.

32

FREE WILL

What a joke! I've brought it up a few times, but let's just spell it out. In the Old Testament free will is a total joke. As most of us know, free will is the idea that you decide what you do. Morally, you know what's right, and you know what's wrong, and you decide whether you are going to do the right thing or the wrong thing. Free will seems to be alive and well in the New Testament, which we'll obviously get to later, but in the Old Testament, not so much. Did Esau and Jacob hate each other, or was it really all God's doing? How about the treachery of Joseph's brothers? What about the Pharaoh? Did he refuse to let the Chosen People go, or was it God hardening his heart? How about Saul? Would he have wanted to kill David if left to his own devices, or was it really that evil spirit from God driving him crazy?

All of this is in addition to the related issue that God determines who wins and who loses all of the wars. If God's with you, you kill the other guy, and if he's against you, you're dead. So where's the freedom? It certainly seems that the very heavy hand of God is often weighing on human affairs, overriding free will and determining outcomes.

Now we see it again with David. God is mad at him for making sure that his lover's husband is killed in battle, so he sends the prophet Nathan to him with a message: Nathan tells David that because of what he's done, God "will raise up evil against you out of your own house."

Right off the bat, God kills the baby David conceived with Bathsheba. Then next thing you know, David's oldest son, Amnon, has the hots for his half sister, Tamar, and he rapes her. Tamar's full brother Absalom hates Amnon for the rape, and subsequently he has his servants kill Amnon. Eventually Absalom turns on David. He leads a rebellion against him, and amazingly the mighty David flees Jerusalem in fear. While he's gone, Absalom comes back to Jerusalem. His counselor, Ahithophel, advises him to publicly humiliate David by having sex with ten concubines his father left behind at his palace. As you might expect, Absalom has no problem with this at all. In fact, he does it in grand style. He puts up a big tent on the roof of the palace and bangs all of the concubines "in the sight of all Israel." Interestingly, we are told that "in those days the counsel that Ahithophel gave was as if one consulted the word of God." It's nice to know that God wanted Absalom to fuck all of his father's whores.

Eventually David rallies, and he defeats Absalom's army. He has told his commanders to spare his son, Absalom, but of course that is not how it works out. Absalom is killed, and God's judgment against David is fulfilled.

Now let's just take a step back here and do a little accounting. We have a dead baby, an incestuous rape, fratricide and rebellion against the father with the rebellion leading to the death of that son as well. When God says he "will raise up evil against you in your own house," he really means it. But the question remains: how are we supposed to understand all of the raping and killing? Did the human beings involved here make any decisions for themselves, or were they all just puppets acting out God's plan?

33

SOLOMON'S SLAVES

I would have thought that by the time Solomon took over as king all of those people who were living in the Promised Land prior to the Chosen People arriving there and who were targeted for removal from their homes and for extermination to make room for said Chosen People would in fact have been exterminated. But apparently a bunch of them were overlooked and somehow survived. For we are told that the slave labor for the temple and the palace that Solomon built was made up of "all of the people who were left of the Amorites, the Hittites, the Perizzites, the Hivites and the Jebusites, who were not the people of Israel—their descendants who were left after them in the land, whom the people of Israel were unable to devote to destruction."

34

SOLOMON AND THE LADIES

In addition to being the smartest guy in the world and the richest guy in the world, Solomon was quite a ladies' man. He had 700 wives and 300 concubines.

Now don't get me wrong. I love the ladies' man thing. But as far as I'm concerned, even one wife is one too many, and 700 wives is just plain crazy—way over the top. I guess if you're King Solomon, you have to have the most wives in the kingdom. It's making sure everybody knows the king has the biggest dick in the kingdom. But I'll bet Solomon could have flipped the numbers and went with 700 concubines and 300 wives and still had the most wives in the kingdom and still gotten credit for having the biggest dick. (Parenthetical note: I've always thought that "concubine" is a very cool word.)

Now the funny thing is that God doesn't care about how many wives or concubines Solomon has. He's totally cool with it. Obviously he changed his mind about this issue some time later. But at this point that's all fine with God. What he doesn't like is not the number of wives or the number of concubines. It's that the women are mostly foreigners. Apparently Solomon just could not get enough of that strange foreign booty. In addition to the Pharaoh's daughter, Solomon was hooked up with Moabite, Ammonite, Edomite, Sidonian and Hittite women. It's all very Freudian since those are pretty much the same people that the Israelites are always wiping out. Apparently the instinctual urges are fully at work here, and it's all about killing and fucking and not much in between.

Anyway, God warned Solomon not to get involved with foreign women. His issue is that they will seduce him into worshipping their gods instead of him, so once again it's all about him. Of course, that is exactly what happens. To please the foreign ladies, Solomon builds altars and worships and sacrifices to a bunch of their gods—to Ashtoreth and Milcom and Chemosh and Molech and probably a ton of others that the Bible doesn't even bother mentioning. And it is this crime that brings a fateful punishment from God. He raises up one adversary after another against Israel, and when Solomon dies and his son, Rehoboam, takes over, the kingdom of Israel is divided in two: Judah, the southern kingdom, composed of two tribes, Judah and Benjamin and ruled by descendants of the House of David; and Israel, the northern kingdom, ruled by the other ten tribes.

35

THE PROPHETS' AMAZING POWERS

Prophets. These are guys who tell you what's going to happen before it happens. They are somehow tapped into God, who knows what is going to happen before it happens and who, as we pointed out previously, appears to intervene quite often to make things happen the way he wants. He does it again when Solomon's son, Rehoboam, takes over for him as king. Since God has decided to punish the people of Israel because Solomon worshipped other gods, he influences Rehoboam to be even harsher with the people than Solomon was, thereby triggering a rebellion, which leads to the division of the kingdom. The old counselors tell Rehoboam to ease up on the people and win their support. The young counselors tell him to hit the people hard. Who does Rehoboam listen to? He listens to the young counselors, of course, despite the callow stupidity of their advice. We are then told that "it was a turn of affairs brought about by the Lord that he might fulfill his word."

In addition to knowing about divine interventions before they occur, prophets have amazing supernatural powers. I think of Moses as the leader of the Chosen People, but you could look at him as a prophet, too. He was always talking to God, so he knew what was going to happen before it happened, and he had amazing powers. Was there ever a more impressive display of supernatural power by a human being than Moses parting the Red Sea? Of course, it was also the first time that anybody parted the waters of a sea or a river. No matter how great something is the second time around it just doesn't seem so impressive. I guess that's why Joshua's amazing feat of parting the Jordan River so the Chosen People can cross into the Promised Land gets so little publicity.

God teaches Moses a whole set of tricks to amaze the people of Israel and the Pharaoh and prove that he has revealed himself to Moses and chosen him as the leader of the people of Israel. Moses learns how to turn his staff into a serpent, how to make his arm turn leprous and then turn healthy again and how to turn the water of the Nile into blood. His brother, Aaron, learns a lot of the tricks, too. Of course, it's when God decides to send one plague after another to punish the Pharaoh for not letting the Hebrew people leave Egypt that we get to see the full scope of Moses's power acting on behalf of God.

The interesting thing is that once the kingdom of Israel is divided, and especially when Ahab becomes king of Israel, there seems to be prophets all over the place. We are told that Ahab "did evil in the sight of the Lord, more than all who were before him." What's more, to show off just how evil he really is, Ahab marries that queen of wickedness, Jezebel, and proceeds to worship Baal, her god of choice. Now we learn that Jezebel has sent her minions through the kingdom to kill all of God's prophets. I don't know how many she killed, but somehow the head of the king's household, Obadiah, has managed to hide 100 prophets in two caves (what a scene that must have been!) On the other hand, we find out later that there are 450 prophets of Baal and another 400 prophets of the goddess, Asherah, working with Ahab and Jezebel. The only prophet still actively representing God is Elijah, but he is really all God needs.

Elijah has skills:

- He can make it rain or cause a drought.

- When he's on the road, the birds bring him food, and if it isn't birds, it's an angel bringing him cakes and water.

- He does his own preemptive turn on Jesus' loaves and fish miracle, albeit for one person; God tells him to go live with a widow and have her feed him and give him water. Only problem is the widow and her son are starving. Elijah tells her that if she helps him out, her jug of flour and her vessel of oil will just keep on replenishing themselves—and they do.

- He can raise the dead. Actually he is the first guy in the Bible to perform this amazing feat, again beating out Jesus by almost 1,000 years. When the widow's son dies, she understandably complains, saying is this how you repay me for my kindness. So Elijah lies down on the dead boy three times, cries out, "Oh, Lord, my God, let the child's life come into him again." And the boy comes back to life.

- He proves that he is more powerful than all 850 of Jezebel's false prophets combined by beating them in a prophet competition.

This last incident also demonstrates what a showman Elijah is. God tells Elijah to go face down King Ahab. When the king sees him, he says, "Is it you, you troubler of Israel." Elijah doesn't even skip a beat. He tells the king he's the troublemaker, and he basically orders him to muster up all of the people of Israel along with the 850 prophets and to meet him up on Mount Carmel for a show-down.

Once everybody is gathered, Elijah berates the entire crowd, saying "How long will you go limping between two different opin-ions? If the Lord is God, follow him; but if Baal, follow him." Then he challenges the 450 Baal guys. He gets a bull, and they get a bull. They both chop up the bull and lay it on some wood. Then they call upon Baal, and he calls upon God to light the fire. Whoever lights the fire is the real God.

The Baal prophets spend the entire morning calling on their god to no avail, while Elijah just watches and laughs. In fact, while the Baal guys are moaning and groaning about not getting a re-sponse, he actually cracks a joke, saying, hey, maybe your god is out taking a piss, or maybe he's asleep. Pretty funny! The Baal guys even try self-mutilation to get Baal's attention, but that doesn't work either.

Finally Elijah builds a proper altar, formally prepares the sac-rifice and calls upon the Lord to show that he is God, and right on cue fire comes down to light the sacrifice. As an encore to this extraordinary performance, Elijah orders the people to seize all 850 false prophets. Elijah leads them down the mountain to a brook and slaughters them all there.

Showing what a wimp he is, Ahab goes running to Jezebel to tell her that Elijah has wiped out all of her guys. Jezebel doesn't mess around. She vows to kill Elijah, and so Elijah heads for the hills. While he's on the lam, he picks up a protégé, Elisha. Eventually Ahab is killed in battle. Dogs lick his blood, as Elijah predicted. Just for good measure, we're told "prostitutes washed themselves in it," too.

Ahab's son, Ahaziah, takes over as king. He somehow falls through a lattice and is in bad shape. He's afraid he's going to die, and like an idiot he sends some men out to ask the god, Baal-zebub, which means "lord of the flies" or "lord of dung," if he is going to get better or not. You have to scratch your head. Ahaziah does this despite the epic humiliation and slaughter of the Baal prophets. Some people just don't learn. God tips off Elijah, and he gets right on top of the situation. He intercepts the king's messengers and sends them back. Then the king sends two different groups of fifty men with their captain, and Elijah brings down fire from God and kills them all. He spares a third group and goes back with them to confront the king. After giving the king a severe tongue lashing, Elijah announces that the king must die, and so he does.

At this point Elijah's work on earth is just about done. He's ready to go to God. And let me tell you. Does he ever know how to make an exit! Just before he leaves, he's walking with Elisha over to the Jordan River. To cap off his brilliant career, he takes off his cloak, rolls it up and hits the water with it. Immediately the waters part, and he and Elisha walk on through. I think here Elijah is showing that he belongs with the greatest miracle workers up to his time—right up there with Moses and Joshua, who were of course the first two guys to part waters.

Right after he does this, chariots of fire and horses of fire fly down out of the sky, separating him and Elisha, and we are told that Elijah "went up by a whirlwind into heaven." When the guys who rebelled against Moses got sent down to Sheol, along with their families, we knew exactly where they went. The earth opened up, swallowed them, and then closed up again. So they basically went down under the ground into a big mass grave. Now in this case, Elijah just sort of disappears, so I really have no idea where he went other than the fact that he went up into the sky. So what we have here is a really theatrical exit by Elijah with the fiery chariots and horses and the Wizard of Oz-like tornado, which is a whole lot better than dying like everybody else has to do, but we still have no idea where heaven is.

In a very classy flourish, Elijah lets his cloak fall down to Elisha as he is being spirited away, signifying that he has literally passed his mantle onto him. Now I can understand that Elisha would really be excited about trying out his new powers right away, but I don't like the fact that as soon as he gets Elijah's cloak, he folds it up, hits the water with it and clears a path for himself right through the Jordan River. I just think that's in bad taste. It's just a "me, too" move and a direct copy of Elijah. And anyway at this point the trick really jumps the shark. I would have much preferred that he do something like walk on the water—just walk on top of the water and go right across the river. If he had done that, he would have really proven something, and he would have aced out Jesus, preempted him with the trick by almost 1,000 years, just as Elijah did when he raised the widow's son from the dead.

The other thing I have to say about Elisha is that he is really thin skinned. One day he's walking along the road and some little kids run up to him and say, "Go up, you baldhead! Go up, you baldhead!" Now that's pretty tame stuff. The kids didn't exactly tell Elisha to go fuck himself, but Elisha gets so annoyed that he conjures up two bears and they come running out of the woods and tear the little boys to pieces. We're actually told that the bears "tore forty-two of the boys." That's quite a crowd of little boys. I just don't know how you explain what happened to all of their parents.

So, as prophets go, Elisha is good, but he's no Elijah. It's like the difference between an all star and a Hall of Famer. A lot of his miracles duplicate or are similar to Elijah's. Even when he raises a boy from the dead, you feel like, OK, I've seen that movie before. Actually he does his most brilliant trick when he's dead. Unlike Elijah, Elisha does not get taken to heaven in a whirlwind. He gets sick and dies just like an ordinary person and is buried in what must have been a rather shallow grave. One day another guy is being buried near Elisha's grave, and a band of crazy marauders comes barreling through the funeral, grabs the dead body and throws it into Elisha's grave. The corpse lands on some of Elisha's bones, which are apparently sticking out of the grave, and just like that, the guy comes back to life. Now that is a good original trick. No way was I expecting that!

36

WHERE'S HEAVEN?

What is it? Where is it? Hard to say.

When it comes to the Old Testament, there's not much talk about heaven. So where did the most important people of the Old Testament go when they died? In the case of all of the earliest people of the Bible—from Adam to Noah—we are simply told how long they lived and that they died. There is no indication that any of them went anywhere after they died. When Abraham, Isaac and Jacob die, we are told that each of them "was gathered to his people," which perhaps means joining one's dead ancestors. What state you're in when you join the dead ancestors—other than dead—isn't really clear. When Joseph dies, we learn that, "they embalmed him, and he was put in a coffin in Egypt." When Moses dies, there is no mention of him going anywhere or even being gathered to his people. In fact, no one even knows where he was buried. When Samuel dies, all we know is that he was buried in his house. Samuel, however, must have gone somewhere. He's called back from the dead by a medium, a woman, who has been hired by King Saul. The Philistines are ready to attack, and he's really worried. God won't talk to him, so he doesn't know what the outcome of the battle will be, but he fears the worst. Saul makes a fool out of himself by going in disguise at night to the woman because of the prohibition against seeking out mediums and necromancers. The woman thinks he's trying to trap her and get her into trouble. Saul asks her to bring up Samuel. When Samuel pops right up, she recognizes Saul, which is rather embarrassing.

Samuel is brought up from somewhere "out of the earth," which sounds an awful lot like Sheol. Anyway when Samuel pops up from down below, he is in a very crabby mood, almost like somebody who has been awakened out of a very sound sleep, and he does not give Saul the answer he was looking for. Samuel reminds Saul that God is mad at him for how he handled the massacre of the Amalekites. He did kill all of the people, as God commanded, so that was good, but he kept the livestock for himself, along with capturing the king as a showpiece rather than killing him and that was not so good. Samuel delivers the very rough news that the next day Saul and his sons will be killed in the battle against the Philistines and join Samuel down under the ground. So maybe the prohibition against mediums was a good idea after all, or at least there should be a warning that you contact the dead at your own risk.

Anyway here's the bottom line: No matter how good or important you were, if you died back in the Old Testament days, you didn't go to heaven. There was no heaven for you. Apparently all you got was a spot to hang out under the ground with all of the other dead people. It was a sort of one-size fits all solution. Everybody went to Sheol. The only exception to this was Elijah—he didn't die. He rode off to heaven in a fiery chariot. I wonder if he was disappointed when he got to heaven and found out he was the only person there. On the other hand, Elijah seemed like a real loner, so maybe he liked it that way.

37

JOB

It's saying a lot, but Job may be the craziest book of the Bible. Revelation gives it some stiff competition, but I think Job is crazier because matter-of-fact craziness beats psychedelic craziness every time.

Let's just take a minute to get the story straight. We're told that "there was a day when the sons of God came to present themselves to the Lord, and Satan also came among them." That sentence alone is enough to make your head spin. Who were these sons of God? Where did they come from? I defy anybody to give me a serious answer to that question. Don't just say they're angels. That begs the question. If you think you have a good answer for who the sons of God are, tweet me. But if you do, I also want to know who their mother is.

Now I know there's been a big discussion going on for centuries about which Satan this is. Is it the real Satan, or is this some other guy with the same name, a guy who's bad and likes to stick it to God when he can but maybe not as bad as the real Satan, the one who turned himself into a serpent in the Garden? Here's what I say. If this guy's got the balls to show up for a meeting at God's house and answer to the name of Satan, then I have to think he's the authentic bad guy—the genuine article.

Now here's the next thing we need to get straight, and it just may be as big a shock as the fact that God has sons. It's clear that God and Satan are on pretty good speaking terms. Sure, there's a lot of history between them, but they just don't seem to be mad at each other at all. In fact, they seem downright friendly. Now whoever wrote the Book of Job is not exactly Elmore Leonard when it comes to dialogue, but God is definitely talking up Satan here. He says, "From where have you come?"

Satan says, "Hey, I've been everywhere, man." You can almost hear Johnny Cash in the background.

Then God says, "Hey, have you seen my man, Job? He's the best guy in the world. He's "a blameless and upright man, who fears God and turns away evil." I love how God always wants everybody to be afraid of him.

In any event, Satan's not all that impressed with Job. He says Job's good because you make sure he has everything. If you start fucking with him and take away what you've given him, he'll hate your guts. In fact, "He'll curse you to your face."

Satan obviously knows how to get under God's skin. God says, let's try that and see. He basically gives Satan carte blanche to fuck over Job. The only restriction is not to hurt him. Now this is really appalling. Not only does God get together with Satan to make Job suffer as a test of his faith and loyalty. He also does it as a kind of bet. Satan is betting that Job cracks under torture, and God is saying, not my guy. No way.

Now when Satan fucks with you, he doesn't mess around. All of a sudden a messenger shows up at Job's house and tells him that a mob descended on his oxen and donkeys and all of the servants tending to them and killed them all except for him. He has miraculously escaped to tell the tale. Two seconds later another messenger shows up and tells Job that fire came down from God and burned up all of his sheep and shepherds, and again the messenger is the lone survivor. Pause two more seconds, and a third messenger comes in to say that another group of bad guys has killed all of Job's camels and the servants tending them. No sooner does this guy arrive then we get even worse news, really the worst news imaginable. A big wind came and knocked down the house where all of Job's sons and daughters were eating and drinking wine, and they're all dead.

In reaction to the loss of his children and all of his possessions, Job tears his clothes off, shaves his head, falls to the ground and worships God, saying, "naked I came from my mother's womb, and naked shall I return. The Lord gave; and the Lord has taken away. Blessed be the name of the Lord." I have a hard time believing that a human being would ever do this. But apparently this is the right response, exactly the one that God was looking for, and we are told that "in all of this Job did not sin," and most important, he "did not charge God with wrong."

Some time passes, and there's another get together with God and his sons, including of course, Satan. God and Satan essentially repeat their conversation from the last meeting. God asks Satan where he's been. He says everywhere. Then God says, hey, how about my guy, Job. He held up pretty well, just as I expected. Amazingly, God blames the killing of Job's children and the destruction of all of his possessions entirely on Satan, saying "he still holds fast his integrity, although you incited me against him to destroy him without reason." He takes no responsibility at all. However, we immediately find out just how easy it is to incite God to destroy Job.

Satan argues that Job remained faithful to God because his health and well-being were not attacked. "But stretch out your hand," he says, "and touch his bone and flesh, and he will curse you to your face."

So, God says, OK. "He is in your hand; only spare his life."

Satan goes right out and afflicts Job "with loathsome sores from the sole of his foot to the crown of his head." At this point Job has just about had it. His wife tells him he should curse God and die. Job remains steadfast in his faith, but makes a very curious remark. After putting down his wife for speaking "as one of the foolish women would speak," he says, "shall we receive good from God, and shall we not receive evil?" Then he grabs a piece of broken pottery to scrape his sores, sits down on the ground in some ashes and doesn't move for a week.

In this wretched state he's visited by three so-called friends. You think they must be pretty good friends because they come and sit down next to Job in the ashes and they stay there in silence with him for a whole week. There aren't too many people who would do that. When Job finally does speak, he's pretty much had it. He curses the day he was born and wishes he had never existed. Since he is alive, he longs for death.

Now if you're a true friend or even a human being with a heartbeat, when you hear this, you would want to acknowledge the legitimacy of your friend's suffering and do whatever you can to try to comfort him. So what do Job's friends do? The first one to speak is a guy named Eliphaz—for some reason Job's friends all have really bad names. He says, hey, Job, whenever bad things happened to other people, you always gave them great advice. You told them to suck it up and keep on keeping on, but now when bad things are happening to you, it's a whole different story. You must know that the innocent are never made to suffer and die. God only punishes the wicked, but no one is blameless. We're all wicked, including you, so this is really all your fault. Put your faith in God, and you'll be just fine and live happily ever after. Pray to him, and he'll make you all better. Listen to me. I'm right, and I'm telling you this for your own good.

Job responds to Eliphaz, saying, I'm talking like this because of how overwhelming and huge my suffering is. What's more, I am praying to God. I'm praying to him to put me out of this misery. I wish I were dead. What kind of a friend are you anyway? You know what I think? I think you're going to be in trouble with God for being so heartless. You want me to shut up, but I'm not going to hold back what I have to say. I'd like to know what I did that was wrong, and if I did do something wrong, why does God take it so personally? Why doesn't he just forgive me and move on? Why is God so obsessed with human beings anyway? And why has he singled out me for torture? My life is hopeless. Why can't God just let me die?

These are amazing questions from Job. They cut right to the heart some of the most important existential issues—why human beings suffer, why bad things happen to good people and why there's evil in the world. Unfortunately Job's friends are totally clueless. Their heads are filled with conventional wisdom and convenient rationalizations. The next friend to speak is Bildad. He has a simple message for Job. Repent! If you forget God, you'll die, but if you repent, he'll restore everything you lost.

Job says, OK. I can repent, but how can I possibly plead my case to God? He's just too powerful. He can make mountains crumble. He can make the earth quake. If he told the sun to stop, it wouldn't rise tomorrow. And anyway, where is he? I've never seen him. If he did stop and talk to me, I wouldn't believe it, and if I did get a chance to plead my case, I wouldn't know what to say even though I know I'm right. In fact, I might find myself admitting guilt even though I'm not guilty just like a guy under torture. Anyway, God "destroys both the blameless and the wicked. When disaster brings sudden death, he mocks at the calamity of the innocent. The earth is given into the hand of the wicked; he covers the face of its judges—if it is not he, then who is it?"

Job states the obvious. There is no one who can represent his cause to God. There is no arbiter, no mediator. How do you go to trial against the judge himself? If you do, you just can't win. But I don't care, Job says. I've got nothing to lose. I'm going to plead my case and ask my questions anyway.

So Job addresses God. He says, what do you have against me, God? You're the one who made me. I didn't ask to be born. You're the one who put me here. You know I haven't done anything wrong. Why do you keep searching for my sin? Why don't you just leave me alone? I'll be dead soon enough anyway.

Now it's the third friend's, Zophar's, turn to speak out against Job. He says, boy, do you have a big mouth, Job. Do you expect us to listen to all of this garbage and not say anything in return? Who do you think you are anyway? I'm going to let you have it because you really deserve it. Do you want to know the truth? You can't take the truth. The truth is if God did speak to you, you would find out that your guilt stinks to heaven. You can't even imagine how guilty you are. You think having your children massacred and losing everything you have is bad? That's nothing. It's beanbag. You deserve worse. God has gone easy on you.

Job says, great. So now I'm also "a laughingstock to my friends." Do you think I don't know what you're saying? I've heard it all before. Look, there's no way around it. God has done this to me. He's the one who has destroyed my life. Nothing happens without him. He's responsible for everything.

Eliphaz pipes up again and says, your problem, Job, is that you don't fear God.

Job says, you guys are the worst friends in the world. Thanks for nothing. I have no hope.

Then Bildad breaks in again and says, I told you already that you're wicked. What do you expect? God punishes the wicked. Shut up and get over it.

At this point Job says, everybody has abandoned me. I'm totally alone and don't tell me that the wicked suffer. The wicked do just fine. He wonders where God is. He still wants to talk to him. Now he's thinking he would like to plead his case on his own and that maybe God would listen to him. But he doesn't know where God is. He can't see him. And, Job says, God doesn't schedule appointments.

At this point a guy by the name of Elihu is introduced. Apparently he's been there listening all along, but nobody bothered to mention him. He's furious at Job's friends and Job too, but he has no problem with God whatsoever. In fact, he is totally on God's side. He says the friends have done a bad job of answering Job, but he'll take care of that himself. Bottom line, he says, God is always just. How could he not be? He's God. He owns all of creation. He could make all living things disappear in an instant. By asserting that he is righteous and that God is making him suffer for no reason, Job is compounding his wickedness with rebellion. God is great. God is inscrutable. Human beings have no right to question him no matter what, so, Job, you should just shut up if you know what's good for you.

Now it turns out that Elihu is a kind of warm-up act for God. He's got all of God's set ups and punch lines down pat. And when he gets to the end of his shtick, who finally appears? It's God, Himself. You can tell it's God because who else would be talking from inside a whirlwind?

God starts out by asking who the idiot is that's making all of this noise. Then he confronts Job, saying I don't remember seeing you around when I created the universe.

God comes across as a classic bully, huffing and puffing about how he can do whatever he wants because he's the boss and he's bigger and stronger than everybody else. But his words are self-indicting. Since he controls all of nature, he is responsible for whatever exists within nature and whatever happens within nature. In other words, whatever exists is God's idea. We can take this a step further and say with confidence that whatever God has created, he thinks it's good. In fact, he says so in Genesis as he admires the workmanship of his own creation. He says: The light is good. The land is good. The seas are good. The fruit and vegetation are good. The stars are good. So are the sun and moon. Fish are good. Birds are good, too. So are all of the animals and insects. Then there's man. He's created in God's image and likeness. He's not as powerful as God, but he's intelligent, capable of reason, and so is God. Man makes choices. So does God. Man has free will when it's not suspended by God. God is free, and there is no one who ever suspends his freedom. So God and man are aligned, and everything that God has created is good.

Here is a list of some of the good things that God has created:

- Hurricanes

- Tsunamis

- Floods

- Land slides

- Avalanches

- Tornados

- Earthquakes

- Volcanic eruptions

- Wildfires

- Lightning strikes

- Droughts

- Blizzards

In a category all by themselves are exploding supernovas and black holes. We don't really care much about exploding supernovas because they are so far away from us. But I hate to think what happens to anybody who is so unfortunate as to live in a zip code nearby. As far as black holes are concerned, I don't know why God thinks they're good since they're like cosmic vacuum cleaners sucking up all of the good God-created stuff that gets too close to them. I wonder if even God knows where all that stuff goes.

It's funny how nobody ever blames God for these natural disasters even though they are all his good ideas. People do pray to God ahead of time. They pray for good things to happen and for bad things not to happen and when bad things do happen, they pray to God to make it all better. Dear God, please help those poor people in Haiti who are suffering so much from the earthquake. Dear God, my daughter has pneumonia. Please make her better. How does that make any sense? Doesn't God already know about Haiti? Doesn't he already know that your little girl is sick? Why do you have to persuade him to help? Also, why do you always have to say I know I don't deserve this God? I'm just not worthy. I'm a miserable sinner. But please be merciful and grant this one request. I promise I'll always be good from now on if you do. I guess when it comes to getting stuff from God a little groveling goes a long way.

I mentioned pneumonia. That brings me to a whole other category of good stuff that God created, namely disease. Here's a partial list of some of the best diseases that God ever created:

- The Black Death

- The Bubonic Plague

- Polio

- Small pox

- Ebola

- E coli

- HIV

- Herpes

- The flu

- Cholera

- Streptococcus

- The common cold

And let's not forget that Bible favorite: leprosy.

In addition to major diseases, there are a number of other conditions that God calls "good." They may not be on the same level of seriousness as the diseases on the list above, but it's still rather curious that God decided to create them and that he calls them "good."

- Male-pattern baldness

- Toe jam

- Hangnails

- Runny nose

- Crotch rot

- Snoring

- Bad breath

- Harelip

- Dandruff

- Acne

- Skin tags

- Bucked teeth

- Hemorrhoids

- Flatulence

- Incontinence

- Benign tumors (That's God just kidding around.)

- Eye floaters

- Erectile dysfunction

If I had the chance to create a universe, it would never occur to me to include any of these things in it. I would never participate in the creation of a nasty universe. Even if I had highly paid advisers who told me that baldness and bad breath were good, I would have just said no. I would have had the courage of my convictions and stood my ground. I would want my universe to be cool and clean, not sick and stinky. I would want no drama and no disease. Viruses and bacteria would be out. Natural disasters? I don't think so. I would have no use for black holes either. But that's just me.

Now God's explanation for all of this is that when he created the world, it was all good and then Adam and Eve ate some fruit that he told them to stay away from and that's how hurricanes and viruses and crotch rot came into the world and that's why people suffer and die. Basically God says, hey, people, don't look at me. It's all your fault.

I just have one word for that explanation: lame. Actually I have another word for it too: dishonest.

What about the issue of evil? People have free will. They can choose to be good or choose to be bad. It's all up to them. As for God, he's all-good. He's got nothing to do with any of the bad stuff. Right? I don't think so. How does the capacity to do evil exist, if that capacity is not within the creator as well? It's just not possible. The fruit that Adam and Eve eat is from "the tree of the knowledge of good and evil." Interesting. So according to Genesis the knowledge of good and evil existed before Adam and Eve ate the fruit and thereby gained access to that knowledge, and if the knowledge of good and evil existed, then good and evil existed as well, and it all came from God, the creator. Obviously.

Also, God didn't have to unleash suffering and death on everybody who ever lives forever and ever until the end of the world because two people ate a piece of fruit. He just felt like it.

Anyway there's nothing sacred about free will. God suspends it any time he wants and actually makes people do bad things to serve his famous higher purpose. Think of Esau and Jacob and Joseph's brothers and the Pharaoh's hardened heart. Remember Flip Wilson's character, Geraldine? She always used to say, "The devil made

me do it." That's not how it is in the Bible. It's always God made me
do it.

If we evaluate God's treatment of Job from a moral standpoint,
we would have to say that it is evil. No way around it. He's torturing
some poor guy to see how he'll react, and he's got a bet going with
another guy just to add a little extra spice to it all. That's sick. But
doesn't God make sure there's a happy ending? Doesn't he restore
everything he took away from Job? After all, he gives him twice as
many livestock as he had before, and Job gets more children too.
Doesn't that make everything OK in the end? No! You got to be
kidding! God doesn't bring back the children that he killed. He just
lets Job have other children over time. Why didn't God bring back
the children he killed? Elijah and Elisha raised the dead. Later on,
Jesus does it, too. What was the problem here? Couldn't God find
Job's children? Or maybe they didn't look so good after the house
fell on them. So God gives Job a new set of children. It reminds me
of the old Dorito's tortilla chip commercial where the guy is sad
that all the tortilla chips are eaten and Jay Leno gives him his goofy
Jay Leno smile and says, "Don't worry. We'll make more."

I guess that's God's answer to Job. I know I killed your children,
Job. But don't worry. We'll make more.

38

WHAT'S THE POINT?

If you're having a hard time getting out of bed in the morning, if you don't want to go to school because it's a drag and your teachers are idiots or you hate your job because it totally sucks and your boss is an asshole, if you're just sort of lying around depressed all of the time and you don't really have any motivation to do anything at all and you're just hanging out playing games on your cell phone and eating salt-based snacks and you finally decide to talk to a friend about your pathetic situation and the friend suggests that maybe you should go read the Bible for some guidance and inspiration, I just have one piece of advice for you: Don't read Ecclesiastes. If you do, you'll go right back to bed and pull the covers over your head. In fact, you might never get out of bed again.

You see, Ecclesiastes will tell you that you were right. It says that "all is vanity." In fact, just a couple of lines in, it says, "What does man gain by all the toil by which he toils under the sun?" At this point you're probably back in bed already, figuring why should I bother reading the rest? Well, you're right. It only gets worse.

Now the speaker is Solomon, so maybe he just got tired of fucking all of those wives and concubines. Whatever the reason, he's decided that he's pretty much seen it all. Been there. Done that.

"What has been is what will be, and what has been done is what will be done, and there is nothing new under the sun."

To put it another way, forget about it, or maybe I should say, whatever you do, no matter how great, nobody will care, for "there is no remembrance of former things, nor will there be any remembrance of later things yet to be among those who come after."

I have to say it's hard to improve on Ecclesiastes. Props to whoever wrote it. From a literary point of view, it's the best thing in the entire Bible. Basically it turns "Life's a bitch and then you die" into poetry.

Now Solomon actually tries to avoid this conclusion. We know he walked down the pleasure trail banging all those bitches, but now after he's done it, he tells us not to bother: "Of pleasure," he says, "What use is it?" On this one, I'm going to part ways with Solomon. Woody Allen once said that sex without love is meaningless, but as meaningless experiences go, it's one of the best, and I'm sticking with Woody on that. But you do have to take into account that the guy talking here is Solomon, and he's the guy who had the most women and the most money and the most possessions, including all the slaves that anybody could want, and he's the smartest guy, too, and he's telling you that everything is just a big waste of time. So if you want to give up, I won't argue with you.

In fact, Solomon really lays it on thick at certain points about the implications of mortality and the futility of existence. Here are a few of his best observations:

"What happens to the children of man and what happens to the beasts is the same; as one dies so dies the other. They all have the same breath, and man has no advantage over the beasts . . . All go to one place. All are from the dust, and to dust all return."

"And I thought the dead who are already dead more fortunate than the living who are still alive. But better than both is he who has not been and has not seen the evil deeds that are done under the sun."

"As he came from his mother's womb he shall go again, naked as he came, and shall take nothing for his toil that he may carry away in his hand."

Now that is some rough stuff. But Solomon doesn't stop there. He has one other major message, and once again I'm reminded of something Woody Allen once said. He used to close his standup act by saying I wish I could leave you with a positive message. I can't. Would you take two negative messages? The funny thing is that Solomon tries to leave us with a positive message after saying that "all is vanity," but it's really just another negative message. His message in the midst of the vanity of life is to "fear God." Does that cheer you up? It doesn't do much for me.

Fear God. Based on everything we've seen of God in the Old Testament, this is pretty good advice. God is jealous. God is angry. God is crazy. If he thinks you're messing around with other gods or doing anything he doesn't like, he'll kill you as soon as look at you—and not just you but your whole family and all of your livestock, too. And these days, you don't even get to go to Sheol, as bad as that was. These days, it's hell for you.

So saying you should fear God is certainly good advice, but somehow I'm just not all that uplifted to learn that we live a totally meaningless existence in which all is vanity and the creator of this world of vanity is a God who we'd better fear, or he'll punish us forever by sending us to hell. Also, if you find yourself thinking that none of this makes any sense and wonder why God would create a world in which all is vanity and in which you are at his mercy every single second, because that just doesn't seem fair, don't bother. Solomon's got that covered. He says that no matter how hard we try, we can never know the mind of God. He has his plan, and we can never presume to understand it. So whatever happens, no matter how bad life gets, no matter how unfair it all seems, accept it. You're just not smart enough to know the real score.

On that note, I think maybe I'll go back to bed, too.

Postscript to Ecclesiastes: I think it's funny that King Solomon tells us to do whatever the king says no matter what; that's rather transparent coming from the smartest guy in the world.

39

PROPHECIES OF THE MESSIAH

Predictions and prophecies are really two different things. If I were predicting that the Phillies will win the World Series this year, I would just say exactly that. Hey, it's the Phillies' year—World Series all the way! If I were to prophesy that the Phillies are going to win the World Series, I would never say that it's going to be this year. That doesn't leave me any wiggle room. What's more, I wouldn't mention the Phillies by name. I might say that a team will come forth from the East and reveal themselves to the world as the champions of all that is good and righteous. That way my prophesy comes true whether the Phillies, Yankees, Red Sox, or, God save us, the Mets win the World Series. If the Rangers or the Dodgers win, that's OK too. All we need to do then is remain faithful and pray that the Day of Judgment and salvation will come in our lifetime.

There are lots of prophecies in the Old Testament about the Messiah, and every single one of them is like my prophecy that the Phillies will win the World Series. Here are a few of the best ones (just to be helpful, in each case I provide a brief interpretation):

"For to us a child is born, to us a son is given; and the government shall be upon his shoulder, and his name shall be called Won-

derful Counselor, Mighty God, Everlasting Father, Prince of Peace."
(Isaiah 9:6) This prophecy says that God will be born as a man.

"Behold, the virgin shall conceive and bear a son, and shall
call his name Immanuel." (Isaiah 7:14) This prophecy says that
the mother of God will be a virgin. It also gives us God's human
name.

"But you, O Bethlehem Ephrathah, who are too little to be
among clans of Judah, from you shall come forth for me one who is
to be ruler in Israel." (Micah 5:2) This prophecy says that the Son of
God will be born in Bethlehem.

"A voice cries: 'In the wilderness prepare the way of the Lord;
make straight in the desert a highway for our God.'" (Isaiah 40:3)
This prophecy says that another prophet will announce the coming
of the Messiah.

"Then the eyes of the blind shall be opened, and the ears of the
deaf unstopped, then shall the lame man leap like a deer, and the
tongue of the mute sing for joy." (Isaiah 35:5-6) This prophecy says
that the Messiah will be a miracle worker.

"I will open my mouth in a parable; I will utter dark sayings
from of old." (Psalm 78:2) This prophecy says that the Messiah will
teach in parables.

"Surely he has borne our griefs and carried our sorrows; yet we
esteemed him stricken, smitten by God, and afflicted. But he was
wounded for our transgressions; he was crushed for our iniquities;

upon him was the chastisement that brought us peace, and with his stripes we are healed." (Isaiah 53:4-6) This means that the Messiah will bear the burden of our sins and make satisfaction to God for those sins by suffering on our behalf.

"He was oppressed, and he was afflicted, yet he opened not his mouth; like a lamb that is led to the slaughter, and like a sheep that before its shearers is silent, so he opened not his mouth." (Isaiah 53:7) This means that the Messiah is the Lamb of God who will suffer silently and be sacrificed for our sins.

"Even my close friend in whom I trusted, who ate my bread, has lifted his heel against me." Psalm (41:9) This prophecy says that the Messiah will be betrayed by a friend with whom he has eaten.

"Then I said to them, 'If it seems good to you give me my wages; but if not, keep them.' And they weighed out as my wages thirty pieces of silver." (Zechariah 11:12) This prophecy says that the price paid for the betrayal will be thirty pieces of silver.

"I am poured out like water and all my bones are out of joint . . . they have pierced my hands and feet—I can count all my bones— they stare and gloat over me; they divide my garments among them, and for my clothing they cast lots." (Psalm 22: 14-18) This prophecy describes the crucifixion of the Messiah.

"And the Lord appointed a great fish to swallow up Jonah. And Jonah was in the belly of the fish three days and three nights." (Jonah 1:17) This means that the Messiah will die and then rise from the dead three days later.

"You ascended on high leading a host of captives in your train and receiving gifts among men, even among the most rebellious that the Lord God may dwell there." (Psalms 68:18) This prophecy says that the Messiah will ascend to heaven.

So you can see—except for the fact they get his name wrong— that without a doubt all of these prophesies are about Jesus and prove that he is the long-awaited Messiah and Son of God.

THE NEW TESTAMENT

40

THE STORY OF JESUS

There's a problem in talking about the story of Jesus. It's a little bit like the problem that physicists have in talking about the universe. Most of it is missing. That's right. In case you didn't know, most of the universe is missing. How much of the universe is missing? Well, actually, just about the whole thing. The latest estimates say that as much as 99 percent of the universe is missing.

Now you might wonder how it's possible that the universe could be so big and most of it be missing. The observable universe is a sphere about 93 billion light years across, and it's expanding. Actually, it's the expansion that revealed this problem. The expansion of the universe is actually speeding up, not slowing down, as crazy as that sounds, and that couldn't be happening unless there was a whole lot more matter out there than anybody has ever found. Scientists call the missing stuff "dark matter." Nobody's ever seen dark matter. You can't see it, but scientists keep looking for it anyway.

When you consider the story of Jesus, you have to admit that although it's viewed by many people as the biggest story of all time with everything depending on it from the meaning of this life to what happens in the next life, including the whole idea of salvation, most of the story is missing. What we do have is not based on any eyewitness accounts, and there are no reliable documentary sources.

Just about everything that we think we know about Jesus comes from the Gospels attributed to Matthew, Mark, Luke and John. Now, maybe you know this, or maybe you don't, but there is just this one little issue about the Gospels that has to be put on the table. It's that they were written decades after the events that they describe, that is to say, decades after the life and death of Jesus. We don't really know who the authors were, but they were clearly followers of Jesus. So the stories are written from the point of view of disciples, advocates, proselytizers. Needless to say, these are not exactly what one would call journalistic accounts. There is no fact checking, no corroboration. So what do we have? Let's take a look.

41

THE BABY JESUS

Nobody doesn't like the Baby Jesus. He's the little tiny baby tucked away in a manger, and he's all wrapped up like a mummy in swaddling clothes. His mother, Mary, is there with Joseph, her betrothed, and you have to think that the real father, the Holy Spirit, is there too even though you can't see him, and then the shepherds who were sent by angels show up to celebrate the birth, and the scene is complete, and it's just a picture perfect little Christmas card. That's the version of Jesus' birth from Luke.

In Matthew's version, there's no heart-warming manger scene at all and no swaddling clothes. We do get the visit from the so-called Wise Men, who follow a star to where the Baby Jesus is, but this is some time after he is born, and they find him at a house. We also get the nasty story of King Herod killing all of the little boy babies to make sure he gets Jesus because he's afraid that he'll grow up to be the King of the Jews. Fortunately, an angel warns Joseph in a dream about Herod, and he and Mary and Baby Jesus flee to Egypt just in time.

Now I would think that if King Herod had ordered his thugs to go out around the time Jesus was born and kill all of the little boy babies, that that would have been a pretty big deal. I wonder why Luke didn't say anything about it. I can understand that he might have thought it would spoil the effect of his picture perfect nativity scene, but still how do you not mention it at all? Maybe he never heard about it in the first place.

In Mark and John, we get nothing. They don't talk about Jesus' birth at all. Either they had no information, or they were just not that interested.

The only other story about Baby Jesus is from Luke. Forty days after Jesus' birth, Mary and Joseph take him to the temple in Jerusalem to present him to God and offer a sacrifice. They encounter an old man, named Simeon. The Holy Spirit has let Simeon know that he will not die until he has seen the "Lord's Christ." He takes Baby Jesus in his arms and says, "Lord, now you are letting your servant depart in peace, according to your word; for my eyes have seen your salvation that you have prepared in the presence of all peoples." What's surprising here is that Mary and Joseph "marveled at what was said about" Jesus. They both seem to have forgotten that Jesus is Christ, the Son of God—this despite the angel Gabriel's annunciation of this message to Mary, the revelation of that message to Joseph in a dream, and all of the angelic hubbub surrounding the visit of the shepherds at Jesus' birth.

With this rather puzzling episode we exhaust all there is to the story of little Baby Jesus. There must have been a whole lot more to it, but it's missing. For example, we don't know if Jesus was a good baby or a bad baby. Did he keep Mary and Joseph up all night crying? Or was it all goo goo and ga ga? When did he first sit up? When did he walk? Did he break any records on those kinds of things? What were his first words? Did he say mama or dada, and if it was dada, whom was he referring to? It would have been nice to know some of these things, but we don't. There's just no information at all.

42

JESUS AS A BOY

What was Jesus like growing up? On this point, Matthew, Mark and John all come up dry. Once again, either they knew nothing about Jesus as a boy, or they didn't think the story was important. Luke has one story—that's right, just one story. And it's a rather puzzling story for a number of reasons. We learn that every year Mary and Joseph go to the temple in Jerusalem for Passover. Jesus is 12 now, and they've just wrapped up their visit and are on the way home. Inexplicably, when they left, Mary and Joseph didn't check to make sure that Jesus was with them and their traveling party of family and friends. He wasn't with them, but they just assumed that he was with somebody else. A day passes before they realize he's not with them. This is all very strange. They go back to Jerusalem, and it takes them three whole days to find Jesus, even though when they do find him, he's at the temple, which is the first place you think they would have looked. When they arrive, Jesus is dazzling everybody with his knowledge. Mary and Joseph are astonished as well, so once again they forget that their young son is the Son of God. If they had remembered this, maybe they wouldn't be so astonished that he knew a thing or two about religion.

When Mary asks her son, "Why have you treated us so . . . your father and I have been searching for you in great distress," Jesus is downright snotty.

He says, "Why were you looking for me? Did you not know that I must be in my Father's house?" OK. So maybe Jesus needs to be in his father's house, but couldn't he have told Mary and Joseph that he was going to stay behind for a few days to hang out and conduct a little seminar with the priests? Would that have been so difficult? If he had done that, he wouldn't have put his mother and father though three days of agony. In fairness to Jesus, after this little outburst, he does submit himself to his parents and return home.

Considering this performance, you have to think that it may be all for the best that we don't know more about Jesus as an adolescent. Truth be told, nobody really likes child prodigies. They just make adults feel stupid. You can tolerate them in small doses, but if you have to put up with them for any longer than, say, ten minutes, you just want to haul off and give them a really good kick in the ass.

43

SOURCES

When a journalist reports a story, the first question the reader asks in trying to determine the story's accuracy and validity is, who were his sources and what did they know first hand? So let's ask that question. Who were Luke's and Matthew's eyewitness sources? Who could they have been? In Luke's version of Jesus' birth, the only people present were Jesus, Mary, Joseph and the shepherds. Jesus was just born, so he doesn't count as an eyewitness. Surely no one believes that the shepherds are the sources. Joseph is never heard from again after the presentation in the temple episode. He disappears. That leaves Mary. She would have had to tell somebody, who told somebody, who told somebody else, and so on and so forth, and then Mary's story, if it ever existed, would have had to find its way through countless retellings to get to Luke maybe 80 years later. How's that for credibility? A similar provenance would have to have occurred in the case of Matthew's story about the Wise Men, although to be precise, Matthew doesn't even include Joseph in the scene. And what about the source for Joseph's dream in which an angel tells him that he doesn't have to be afraid to take Mary as his wife because she was impregnated by the Holy Spirit and not some unknown guy? Where did that story come from?

Who's the source for the story about the devil tempting Jesus in the desert? Would that be the devil or Jesus? What about the account of Jesus praying by himself in Gethsemane while the apostles sleep? What about the account of Jesus being questioned by Pontius Pilate? Who relayed that exchange to the gospel writers? Benefit of the doubt? I don't know. Maybe there was a mole in the Pontius Pilate organization.

You can ask these same questions about every single story in all four of the gospels. Even when the disciples or other named people are with Jesus, there is no way of knowing if the events described ever occurred. If any of the events described did occur in some way, shape or form, there is no way of knowing what portion of the description of the events is accurate. Apparently divine inspiration covers a multitude of journalistic sins.

44

JOHN THE BAPTIST

John the Baptist is a little bit scary. He wears camel's hair, which has to be really hot and itchy, especially out in that horrible desert heat. All he eats are locusts and wild honey (even he won't eat locusts without sweetening them up a bit), and he's one of those preternaturally angry preachers, the "voice crying in the wilderness," calling out the archetypal message—"Repent, for the kingdom of heaven is at hand."

But his words are the most intimidating thing about him. He gets in the face of the Pharisees and Sadducees, the phony philosophers and politicians, who show up to spy on him when he preaches. The good news he is preaching is not good news for them.

It would be interesting to know John's thoughts. He's the one who prepares the way for one who is greater than he, but that one declares, "Among those born of women there is no one greater than John the Baptist."

In his iconic baptism of Jesus, the spirit descends like a dove and a voice from heaven says, "This is my beloved Son with whom I am well pleased." It is the voice of God, and in that moment there is a seismic dislocation. This is the voice of God, but it is markedly different from the voice that spoke to Moses from a burning bush.

God has changed, or it is a different God. This God is fatherly and closer to human for now having a human son.

With the baptism, John eclipses himself. Fearless and doomed, with his mission nearing its end, he must have known his life would soon be over.

It would be interesting to know John's thoughts, interesting to know if he thought his head would end up on a plate.

45

THE DEVIL TEMPTS JESUS

Maybe he was just having a bad day, but I have to say that in his temptation of Jesus, the devil was not just insulting, which you might expect, but stupid as well. It's hard to believe that this is the same guy who answered to the name, Satan, and who made the bet with God to fuck over Job. He doesn't seem as sharp, but again maybe he was just having a bad day.

Jesus has been hanging out in the desert for forty days and forty nights. He hasn't eaten a thing, and it's a miracle that he's still walking around and talking. The devil comes up to him at this very vulnerable moment and tempts him three times. The story has a little bit of an Old Testament feel to it because we're told, "Jesus was led by the Spirit into the wilderness to be tempted by the devil." So once again God, in this case the Spirit, wants to test a human being to see whether or not he will remain loyal to him. Only in this case the human being is Jesus, who is God, so he's sending himself out in the desert to see if he as a human being will remain faithful to himself as God.

Confusing? Not a bit.

Anyway the devil must have been watching Jesus. He knows Jesus is really hungry, so the first thing he does is tempt him with food. He says, "If you are the Son of God, command these stones to

be loaves of bread." What's insulting here is that the devil is acting incredulous over the fact that Jesus is the Son of God, and he's
telling him to prove he is by doing a magic trick. Once again you
have to wonder if this is the same guy as Satan in the Job story,
even though after the last temptation, Jesus actually refers to him
by that name. That Satan seems to drop by God's house any time he
wants. You'd think that if he were Satan, he would have gotten word
already that God had sent his Son down to earth. Who knows?
But why does the devil think if Jesus turned stones into bread and
started eating the bread stones it would prove that he's the Son of
God? I'll bet that Moses or Elijah or even Elisha could have done
that trick in their sleep. They all did water and food tricks back
in the day. So the devil's not just being insulting here. He's being
downright stupid, too.

When this ham-handed temptation doesn't work, the devil suddenly transports himself and Jesus out of the desert. Now they're in
Jerusalem, and they're standing on the "pinnacle of the temple," and
the devil tells Jesus to jump off. Right. Jesus is going to jump off the
roof of the temple, land on his feet like an alley cat—no harm, no
foul—and yell back up at the devil, "Take that fuck face! Now you
try it!"

So that brilliant temptation doesn't work either. At this point
the devil must be getting pretty desperate. Now suddenly Jesus
and the devil are standing on top of a high mountain—they really
do get around—and the devil shows Jesus "all the kingdoms of the
world," and he says, "'All of these I will give you if you fall down and

worship me." I'm sorry but this is the stupidest fucking temptation of all. This would be like somebody standing with me in front of my house and saying, I'll let you live here if you kiss my ass. I already do live here, shit for brains. Now get the fuck out of my face.

I remember reading this when I was a kid and saying to myself, what's the devil thinking? Jesus already owns the whole joint.

At this point, Jesus has had enough. He says, "Be gone, Satan!" which I always liked. I've always wanted to tell somebody to be gone. It just sounds cool. I also like that as soon as the devil leaves, angels come rushing over to Jesus to minister to him sort of like a boxer's seconds in the ring after a round where their guy just totally kicked ass.

46

JESUS, THE MIRACLE WORKER

Some people call the 18 years about which nothing is written about Jesus the "silent years." We simply have no information at all on this extended period of Jesus' life.

The last glimpse we have of Jesus at the temple when he was 12 is intriguing. We see a young boy who abandons his parents and goes off on his own without regard to their feelings and who exhibits more than a little attitude when they ask him why he put them through such worry and heartache over his disappearance. We see a precocious teacher and preacher in the making, and naturally we wonder about how he developed over those many years.

How, for example, did Jesus become a miracle worker? Did he just wake up one day and perform his first miracle? Did he have to practice? Did his early miracles always go well, or were there some embarrassing failures? I wonder if Jesus had a sort of Harry Potter period where he was learning to be a miracle worker. I really doubt that he started right off driving out demons or raising the dead.

Actually there are a couple of neat tricks that Elisha performed that would have served as good practice for a miracle-working apprentice. Now I'm not sure how the first one even got into the Bible, but I'm glad it did. It's so ridiculously trivial that it's funny. There was a group of guys who followed Elisha around called the Sons of the Prophets. For some reason Elisha had the Sons of the Prophets all living in the same house. One day, they went to Elisha and told him that the house was too small for them. I don't know how many of them there were, but I bet they had a point. It must have been really crowded and slummy. Anyway they wanted to build a new house, and Elisha said, go right ahead. So the sons started chopping down trees to build a new log house. As they were working away, an axe head fell into some water. This is not exactly the end of the world, but the guy got all bent out of shape because he had borrowed the axe. Right away, though, Elisha comes to the rescue. He asks him where the axe fell, cuts off a branch from a tree, throws it there, and ta-da! The axe head floats right to the surface.

I can imagine Jesus trying out this trick around Joseph's carpenter shop. Maybe Jesus would walk around all day with a stick in his hand just hoping that something would get lost so that he could throw the stick in the right direction and find it—it could be a hammer, a box of nails—I don't know, anything. Maybe one day Joseph misplaced one of his sandals, and Jesus threw his stick, and there it was. I wish I knew how to do this trick because I'm always losing my cell phone.

The other trick of Elisha's that would have really been good for a young miracle worker to practice on is the one where he purifies the deadly stew. If I were editing the Bible, this is another trick that I would have just left on the cutting room floor, but it's in there, and I'm sure that Jesus, as a young biblical scholar and teacher, knew all about it. Who knows? Maybe it was put in there by God just for him—another good little trick to practice on around the house to hone his miracle making skills before he went prime time.

The story of the deadly stew revolves around another Sons of the Prophets screw up. Elisha tells his servant to make some stew, and one of the sons runs outside and collects some herbs and wild gourds and throws them into the stew. If I had seen that, there's no way I would have eaten that mess, but the servant cooks it all up and serves it to the sons. The guys are eating away when all of a sudden one of them screams, "O man of God, there is death in the pot!" I guess the gas pains were kicking in pretty good.

Anyway Elisha knows exactly what to do. He has the servant get him some flour. He throws the flour into the pot and voilà! He turns the poison stew into the best stew you could ever want to eat.

Now I'm sure at one time or another Mary might have cooked up something—maybe a goat stew or a vegan dish of herbs and gourds like the sons did—and while it might not have been poison, it was just not up to snuff. Maybe Joseph would give Jesus a little look, and Jesus would look back and then when Mary left the room, Jesus would grab some flour, throw it into the stew and turn what would have been a disaster of a dinner into the culinary master-piece of the week. "Wow! This is great stew, Mom," Jesus might say when Mary came back into the room, and Joseph would smile and give his boy a little fatherly pat on the back.

Close-up magic tricks involving food or drinks are always a big hit. The best trick I ever saw was performed by a magician one

night at the Waldorf Astoria in Manhattan. He had everybody
in the audience write down their favorite drink on a little piece
of paper. His assistant collected the pieces of paper, and then she
began opening them up one by one. The magician had a teapot in
his hand. When the assistant read out the name of a drink, he asked
whose drink it was, and then he and his assistant came over to that
person and poured that drink out of the teapot and gave it to the
person. That guy poured chocolate milk, orange juice, Chardonnay
and a martini right out of that same teapot all in a row. That was
amazing. I still have no idea how he did that.

Jesus really liked performing miracles involving food or drink.
According to John, Jesus' first public miracle was turning water
into wine. This also happens to be my favorite Jesus miracle of all.
Everybody knows this story. Jesus is at a wedding with Mary. They
run out of wine, and Mary tells Jesus. Clearly she expects him to do
something about it, and it's not run to the local wine store. This tells
me that he's been doing miracles and tricks around the house for a
long time, and she knows he can handle this no wine situation with
his eyes closed.

Jesus, however, gets annoyed. He's actually pretty grouchy with
his mother just the way he was at the temple when he was 12, so
apparently the attitude thing never went away. Jesus says, "Woman,
what does this have to do with me? My hour has not yet come."

Funny thing is, Mary just ignores him. No doubt, she's handled
Jesus and his attitude lots of times before. She just turns to the ser-

vants and says, "Do whatever he tells you." So Jesus is on the hook to fix the situation compliments of Mom.

Jesus tells the servants to fill all of the jars they have with water. There are six jars, which we're told hold "twenty or thirty gallons." For some reason John doesn't know exactly how big they were. Either way, though, that's a lot of water and a lot of wine. The servants fill the jars to the brim and take a sample to the master of the feast. He tastes the water, and of course it's now been turned into wine—pretty good wine, too.

As the master famously says, "Everyone serves the good wine first, and then when everyone has drunk freely, then the poor wine. But you have kept the good wine until now."

As we know, Jesus does a couple of totally amazing food miracles, too. He wasn't the first, of course. The Old Testament God rained down manna on the Chosen People every day for forty years, and it's hard to beat that. Elijah and Elisha did food tricks, too, but they were always small-scale, in-the-home type tricks. As I've already mentioned, Elijah turns a widow's jar of flour and jug of oil into the gifts that keep on giving. They just keep producing flour and oil every day until the next time it rains. There was a terrible drought going on because God was punishing the evil King Ahab. I'll bet the widow was sad when the rains finally came.

Elisha helps out a widow, too. I guess back then widows were first in line to get help from the big time prophets. This particular widow's dead husband left her owing money to some guy. I don't know how much money it was, but it must have been a lot because when the widow tells him she can't pay, he wants her to give him her two children as slaves. All the widow has is a jar of oil to give the guy, so it's a pretty sure thing that he's going to take the kids instead. Elisha tells her to borrow jars of oil from all of her neighbors. She gets a hold of tons of empty jars, brings them into her house and just goes crazy filling every single one with oil from the one jar she already has. There's so much oil that she's able to pay off the would-be slave trader and live off of the money from the rest of the oil.

So these are definitely a couple of good tricks, but they're kind of laid-back and down-home, unplugged, if you will. Jesus taps into the concept of the food miracle, but he takes it to a whole new level. In two absolutely amazing performances, he feeds huge crowds even though there is almost no food. In one case, he feeds 5,000 people with just five loaves of bread and two fish. In the second instance, he feeds 4,000 people with just seven loaves and a few fish. What I like most about these miracles is that Jesus provides so much food from a few loaves of bread and a couple of fish, there are actually leftovers. In fact, both times there are baskets of food left over. That means doggy bags for the apostles and Jesus when they hit the road.

The coolest miracle that Jesus ever performed has to be when he walked on water. I mean here he's suspending the laws of gravity and the curvature of space, and I'll bet he didn't even get his sandals wet. Jesus lets Peter walk on water, too, as long as he has faith, which of course lasts about ten seconds.

Most of Jesus' miracles had to do with healing people, and this was the best thing about Jesus. He cared if you were hungry, and he cared if you were broken down or sick, and if you believed in him, he was always happy to feed you or make you better. He makes the mute speak, the lame walk and the blind see. I especially like the time that two blind guys called out to Jesus from the side of the road and the crowd following Jesus told them to shut the fuck up. Jesus stopped anyway, took pity on them and gave them back their sight.

Jesus also cast out a lot of demons. Back then, there were apparently a lot of people who were possessed by demons. My favorite casting-out-demons story takes place right after Jesus just calmed a storm—another one of his best miracles. He's just stepped out of the boat, and he sees a possessed guy coming at him from out of some tombs, which is evidently where he lived. The guy is really crazy, and he can't even be held down by chains, which is apparently the therapy that he had been prescribed. He's so strong, he just breaks the chains and runs around the tombs and up and down the mountains all day and all night, screaming and mutilating himself with stones.

The guy must have been pretty intimidating, but Jesus doesn't even blink. He just starts talking to the head demon inside of the guy, ordering him and all of his demon friends to come out. Somehow, there's a herd of about 2,000 pigs nearby, and the head demon decides he wants Jesus to send him and his friends into the pigs. I have no idea why, but, hello, the demons are just plain crazy. Jesus says, you got it, pal, and the demons go flying—just like that—into the pigs. Instantly, the pigs go crazy, run down a steep bank and drown themselves in the sea. Pretty cool, to say the least, except for the pigs.

Of course, Jesus' greatest miracles have to do with raising the dead. Lazarus is the best-known example, but he also brings back to life a little girl and a boy. Elijah and Elisha also raised the dead, so Jesus wasn't the first one to do it, but he totally outdoes them with the greatest miracle of all—the resurrection. Jesus raises himself from the dead, and there's just no topping that.

47

Jesus Is Cool

There may not be much competition for cool in the Bible, but there is no doubt that, taken as a human being, Jesus is the coolest guy by far. Now I have to say that thinking you're God and being cool normally runs counter to one another. There are very few people with high opinions of themselves who are cool. Just about zero. But that's just it. If you are the smartest fucking guy in the room and you think you are, what of it? What else would you think? You are that guy. So long as you know that there are a lot of other rooms with smart guys in them and it doesn't matter anyway, you're cool.

Jesus is God. It is what it is, and he is who he says he is. So there!

The only thing that's cool in the Old Testament is Ecclesiastes. Life's a drag, man. Don't Bogart that joint. Otherwise, nothing is cool. Certainly not God.

The OT God never cries. When John the Baptist is murdered, Jesus goes off by himself to a desolate place. When Lazarus dies, Jesus cries even though he's going to bring him back to life ten minutes later. That's cool.

The OT God and the OT leaders and prophets are all about rules. Jesus is about the spirit. Spirit is cool. Rules are not.

The OT God's idea of being kind and compassionate to the Chosen People is giving them bread and water—as in manna and the water flying out of the rock—during their solitary confinement in the desert. Jesus turns water into wine. He walks on water. He calms the waters. Water comes out of his side right after he dies.

The OT God does not allow anyone who is disabled or broken down in some way to approach his altar. Jesus welcomes you.

The OT God is a tester and a jester—only he's not funny. Jesus is a healer. He cures people of disease and makes the broken whole. He feels their pain.

The OT God appears with lightning and thunder. Jesus calms the storm.

Jesus hangs out with lowlifes.

Jesus is into the women, working girls included.

Jesus loves children.

Jesus hangs with tax collectors too, so even if you're from the IRS, you won't freak him out.

Jesus has answers for every trick question.

Jesus can be gentle, but he's right in your face if the situation calls for it.

Jesus is for the laborer and those who are "heavy laden." He promises rest.

That's Jesus, and that's cool.

48

THANK YOU, JESUS

So Jesus was a very cool guy. I think we should thank him for being so cool. Here are some of the things that I'd like to thank him for.

Thank you, Jesus, for turning water into wine.

Thank you, Jesus, for healing the man with dropsy on the Sabbath. Nobody knows what dropsy is, but it must be bad (actually it's water retention), and you healed the man (where did the water go?) even though it was the Sabbath, and you told the lawyers and the Pharisees who thought that you should wait until the next day to heal him to shove it because they were such hypocritical assholes.

Thank you, Jesus, for hanging out with shady people. Shady people are the best company.

Thank you, Jesus, for saying, "The last will be first, and the first last."

Thank you, Jesus, for advocating the Golden Rule.

Thank you, Jesus, for saying, "Blessed are the peacemakers."

Thank you, Jesus, for saying "Whoever is not with me is against me."

Thank you, Jesus, for calling out the hypocrites.

Thank you, Jesus, for your love of children and for saying that if anyone harms a child, "It would be better for him to have a millstone fastened around his neck and to be drowned in the depths of the sea."

Thank you, Jesus, for weeping over the death of Lazarus.

Thank you, Jesus, for expecting nothing in return.

Thank you, Jesus, for not judging.

Thank you, Jesus, for being fearless.

Thank you, Jesus, for saying that "The truth will set you free."

49

THE PARABLES DECODED

We all know the parables. They're tiny little stories that make a point or teach a lesson through analogy. But what's really interesting about the parables is that Jesus saw them as a way of speaking in code. If you were a believer, if you were on his team, you understood the code—at least some of the time. If you were an unbeliever who was out to get him, like the Pharisees and Sadducees, you didn't understand the code, and if you thought that maybe you heard something that you could hold against Jesus, you were out of luck because he had deniability. After all, he was only talking about a mustard seed or fig trees or the lilies of the field.

Here are a few of the parables decoded:

The Mustard Seed: The smallest thing may become the greatest thing. Think: a Planck-sized nugget explodes into the universe; a decision changes a life; an idea changes the world.

The Pearl of Great Price: A single thing that truly matters is worth more than everything that does not matter. Think: a son or a daughter; the right to be yourself; the freedom to offend.

The Good Samaritan: The true and loving one, the generous and giving one, may be the one that you despise. Think: the foreign one; the ugly one; the strange one, the one you would never consider, the outsider—the "other."

The Prodigal Son: Celebrate the return of the one who was lost. Think: forgive without remembering; love without conditions; "home is where the heart is."

The Lilies of the Field: "Do not be anxious about your life." Think: follow your dream; live each moment; "hey, ho, the wind and the rain."

50

THE BAD GUYS

Who are the bad guys? There's a pretty long list. They're the Pharisees, the Sadducees, the scribes, the high priests, the elders and the lawyers. The Roman politicians are bad guys too, although they're secondary. The interesting thing is that we know a lot of these guys firsthand because in one form or another they're still around today. They're everywhere really:

They're the ones who know they're saved and hope you're not.

They're the voice of the institution, dictating what's wrong and what's right.

They're the hypocrites who do as they please when they're out of sight and behind closed doors.

They're the politicians who tell you what you want to hear but believe nothing themselves.

They're the politicians who want the economy to stay bad.

They're the politicians who say they have a plan but won't tell you what it is.

They're the ones who won't answer the question you ask them but give you a speech instead.

They're the ones who choose laws and rules over people.

They're the ones who look down on good works.

They're the ones who want to trip you up and put you on the spot.

They're the ones who show up, hoping to see you fail.

They're the ones who think they win when other people lose.

They're the ones who are so stupid, they think they're smart.

They're the holier than thou bigots.

They're the users.

They're the abusers.

They're the ones who would kill you if they could.

51

DOES JESUS THINK HE'S GOD?

In a word, yes. He says that he is in many ways and at many times. When messengers from the jailed John the Baptist ask Jesus, "Are you the one who is to come, or shall we look for another?" he references his miracles as signs that he is the one, i.e., the Messiah, the Son of God.

He says, "Go and tell John what you hear and see: the blind receive their sight, the lame walk, lepers are cleansed and the deaf hear and the dead are raised up."

When the Samaritan woman says to him, "I know that the Messiah is coming (he who is called Christ). When he comes, he will tell us all things," Jesus replies, "I who speaks to you am he."

When Jesus asks his disciples, "Who do you say I am?" Peter replies, "You are the Christ, the Son of the Living God," and he names Peter the head of his church and orders them not to tell anyone that he is the Christ.

When the devil tempts him, he tells him, "You shall not put the Lord your God to the test."

Of course, when he's in front of his human enemies, he never gives them exactly what they want. In fact, he can be downright elusive. When the Pharisees and Sadducees demand a sign from heaven, a miracle, he refuses to put on a show for them, saying you're good at predicting the weather from signs in nature, "but you cannot interpret the signs of the times."

When the high priests and elders ask him by what authority he teaches, Jesus says he'll tell them if they will tell him whether the baptism of John came from heaven or from man. When they refuse to answer, Jesus refuses to answer them as well.

When he's questioned by the high priests and scribes after his arrest and they say to him, "If you are the Christ, tell us," Jesus replies, "If I tell you, you will not believe, and if I ask you, you will not answer, but from now on the Son of Man shall be seated at the right hand of the power of God."

When they ask in response, "Are you the Son of God, then?" Jesus says, "You say that I am." When Pilate asks him, "Are you the King of the Jews?" Jesus says, "You have said so."

Jesus' consciousness of being God is constant, but the remarkable thing about him is that he's constantly human as well. He's caring and compassionate. He heals; he cures; he relieves the suffering of others. He's generous. He's patient. He always has time for a person in need, even though he can also get annoyed with his mother and family if they fail to defer to him in pursuing his ministry.

There is, however, one thing missing. Jesus doesn't seem to have a sense of humor, but maybe Matthew, Mark, Luke and John just left that out.

52

NOBODY'S PERFECT

Guess who talks about hell and damnation a lot? Jesus. That's right. Jesus. It may seem out of character, but he does.

I guess nobody's perfect.

Jesus says that hell is a fiery furnace. He says that if your hand or your foot get you into trouble, you should cut them off, and if your eye gets you into trouble, you should pluck it out. Wow! Can you imagine what shape you'd be in if your hands and feet and eyes all got you into trouble and you followed Jesus' advice? Let's just say that I think you'd qualify for 100 percent disability. But Jesus says you'd be better off as an eyeless guy with no hands and no feet than to be one of those godforsaken people who are "thrown into hell, where their worm does not die and the fire is not quenched. For everyone will be salted with fire." I think the "worm" reference here has to do with fireproof maggots—but enough said about that.

I could go on, but I won't. There are tons of references. Matthew, Mark, Luke and John all make sure that Jesus talks about hell all of the time. I'm sure they were all into hell big time.

The funny thing is how many people today are still into hell. All these years later there are actually lots of people who seem to like this side of Jesus the best. They love hell, and they absolutely love and cherish every single time that Jesus talks about it. They're glad he's pretty nice the rest of the time, too, except when he's in the face of the Pharisees and the Sadducees and the other bad guys or the time he kicks all of the entrepreneurs and small business people out of the temple. The logic is that Jesus is the most loving and forgiving guy of all time, and even he is telling you that if you don't change your evil ways, you are going to hell.

One thing for sure, the people who like the hell talk side of Jesus best—they would certainly send you to hell. Happy to do it. They would send you there for just about anything. Back in the day, they were the ones who would send you there if you ate a baloney sandwich on Friday. Or if you had an impure thought—just a little black and white snapshot of a booby slipping its way into your brain. That's all it took, and you were toast.

There's no way to get around it. Hell may just be the single best idea in the entire history of religion. It's certainly one of the most popular ideas. Egalitarian too, because, if you think about it, hell is one of the very few opportunities available to everyone. We all qualified for hell on the day we were born.

53

JESUS FLIPS OUT

Why do you flip out on one day and not another? I'm talking here about people who are generally very calm and self-controlled, not all those angry little puppy dogs and out-of-control bullies who rant and rave on a daily basis, abusing anybody who gets in their way. Just what happens? Do you wake up that day primed for a flip out? Did some trigger mechanism go off in your sleep? Was it a dream that set it off? Is it the result of some cumulative build up of stress and anxiety? Or is it spontaneous? Does somebody just push the wrong button on you, and you go off like a maniac, just like that?

I wonder what the explanation is in Jesus' case. We all know his famous flip-out scene. Out of the blue he storms into the temple, makes a whip out of some cords and drives out everybody who is selling stuff and doing financial transactions. Just how many people did he singlehandedly drive out of there? I know we're talking about Jesus here, but I've always wondered how he did that? How was it that he got everybody to leave and didn't get his ass kicked? He must have come on like superman. He not only drives people out. He drives out the sheep and oxen too. Now I have to agree with Jesus on kicking the animals out. If there were livestock in a temple or a church, I sure as hell wouldn't go inside.

Jesus also knocks over all of the tables and throws the money up in the air and tells off the pigeon sellers, too. Here again I say, good for Jesus. I wouldn't want pigeons in my church either or the people who are selling them, and who buys pigeons anyway? It's clear that the enterprising characters he kicked out had turned the temple into a kind of bazaar or primitive mall. I just wonder again what made him go nuts that day and not some other day. Maybe in his case it was strategic. Maybe it was all planned out, and this was just the perfect time to go crazy and drive all of the assholes out of the temple.

As soon as they're gone, Jesus is back to his old self. He lets in the blind and the lame and heals them. Apparently he was able to go nuts without scaring any of the children. In fact, the kids must have gotten a kick out of it because now there are a bunch of them in the temple cheering for him, crying out, "'Hosanna to the Son of David!' This really pisses off the chief priests and the scribes. They always hate it whenever anybody says that Jesus is the Messiah.

I like that the Gospel writers describe this scene as Jesus cleansing the temple. Can you imagine if you somehow put on a superman act at a local bar and drove all of the riff raff out of the place and when the cops came, you told them you were cleansing the bar? I bet they wouldn't expect that.

Postscript to Jesus Cleansing the Temple: The morning after Jesus cleanses the temple (actually that's Matthew's version; Mark says it was the day before), Jesus comes upon a fig tree and wants to pick some figs and eat them. When it turns out that the poor fig tree doesn't have any figs, Jesus blasts it and the tree withers and dies on the spot. Ouch! I really do not know what set off Jesus right around this time, but I'm sure that if I were one of his disciples, I would have just stayed the fuck out of his way until the whole thing blew over.

54

Jesus Rejected in His Hometown

I like this little story about how when Jesus went back home to Nazareth, a bunch of his friends and neighbors immediately turned against him, saying who does he think he is to be acting so smart? We know where he comes from. We know his family. He's no better than we are. Shockingly, in Luke's version Jesus is driven by a mob out of the town to the edge of a cliff. As his friends and neighbors are about to throw him off, he magically "passes through their midst" and leaves Nazareth behind.

Remember this story, boys and girls, if you leave home, go out on your own and then come back home for a visit after you've had some success somewhere else, especially if you've made a little money. If you think everybody is going to be proud of you and happy for your success, think again. Some people will, but a lot of your old pals will be jealous of you because you make them feel like the losers they are.

There have been losers everywhere throughout history. Losers only like other losers. They don't like winners. The losers are the ones putting down Jesus, and they'll do the same thing to you. So watch your back.

I'm just sayin'.

Postscript to Jesus Rejected in His Hometown: Jesus is forgiving as we all know, but he makes a point of getting back at the jealous homeboys. He tells them "a prophet is not without honor except in his hometown and in his own household." Then he takes his show on the road and freezes them out. Indeed, we are told, "He did not do many mighty works there, because of their unbelief."

55

BETRAYAL

You can't have betrayal without trust. If there was never any trust, then the person who's doing you wrong is just fucking you over, which is about par for the course. Betrayal is a whole different matter. It means your father or your mother or your brother or your sister or your best friend or your next-door neighbor or your business partners or your boss or your colleague at work or your teacher or a priest or a minister or a rabbi has turned on you and violated the whole basis of their relationship with you. They've gone and done something that just cuts you in two—cheated on you, lied about you, put you down to your face, put you down behind your back, took the side of your enemies, remained silent while somebody else was betraying you, beat you, abused you, molested you, plotted against you, maybe even tried to kill you—the list goes on and on.

The amazing thing is just about everybody has been betrayed. It's hard to get through life without it happening to you. And the amazing thing, too, is that the Bible tells you to expect it. He's kind of hard to like, but sometimes you have to feel a little bit bad for the OT God because the Jewish people, the people that he chose, are betraying him all of the time, always cheating on him, always worshipping some other god. He tends to overreact, but you have to admit that he does get the shaft from his people quite a bit. I've talked about brothers betraying one another—it goes all the way back, of course, to Cain and Abel. There are also the stories of Delilah and Samson; David and Uriah, Bathsheba's husband; Absalom and David—not to mention God and Job. Those stories just say, watch out. You can't trust anybody. As David says in Psalm 55:

It is not an enemy who taunts me—

then I could bear it;

It is not an adversary who deals insolently with me—

then I could hide from him.

But it is you, a man, an equal,

my companion, my familiar friend.

There is nothing worse than betrayal, but the ultimate story of betrayal, hands down no competition at all, is the story of Jesus. He's the best guy that ever was, and he's the Son of God, too, and in the end, he's betrayed by just about everybody.

56

Killing Jesus

The humanity of the story continues to resonate. You are betrayed by a kiss from one of your closest friends. You knew it was coming, but it's a shock when it happens nonetheless. Maybe it's even a bigger shock when you know it's coming. Maybe when you experience the moment in which that foreknowledge is fulfilled, it hurts more than you imagined, and you are stunned. So there, you say. The kiss. Now it is done, and now the rest will follow.

When the mob comes to arrest you, Peter grabs a sword and cuts off the ear of one of the assailants, but that's not what you want. You restore the ear, and the mob takes you away.

In the blink of an eye Peter denies you three times as you told him he would; the cock crows and you remember his denial of the denial.

You face your accusers and inquisitors alone. For the longest time you remain silent in the face of false accusations and insults. Finally you are asked if you are the Son of God and you reply, "You have said so." You are accused of blasphemy, and they call for your death. They spit at you and slap you.

Later Pilate asks you if you are the King of the Jews, and again you reply, "You have said so," and go silent. The mob is given a choice—to release you or a criminal. They choose the criminal.

You're beaten, crowned with thorns and dressed in a purple robe. The crowd cries out, "Crucify him."

You carry the cross to the place of execution. It is called Golgotha, a Place of the Skull. It is all happening as planned.

Everyone you loved and trusted is gone except your mother, Mary; her sister, Mary; your friend, Mary Magdalene; and just one of your 12 apostles, John. You feel abandoned, even by God, your Father, and cry out, "My God, my God, why have you forsaken me?"

The Son of God, human to the end, you cry out one last time and die, fulfilling your divine mission.

57

JESUS IS BACK

We've all been in bad situations where we just wanted to find the way out. Bad scene, bad news, bad directions, bad flight, bad job, bad marriage, bad divorce, bad deal, bad dream, bad day. Just bad. So bad, it can't get any worse. Or can it?

When you're dead, that's pretty darn bad. You got nothing going on any more. Thank God, Jesus shows us the way. You just pick yourself up and rise from the dead. What's stopping you?

When the women arrive, he is already gone. There's an angel there instead or maybe two. So the ladies go out to spread the news. Jesus is back.

Actually the Gospel guys have a hard time getting their notes straight on what exactly happened after Jesus rose from the dead. The gist though is that the women believe he has risen and the men don't except for Peter and John in John's version. They actually take the trouble to go out to the tomb and find it empty.

Unbelievable! How many times did Jesus tell the apostles that he was going to rise from the dead after three days? You'd think they would have been camped out waiting for him and have given him a standing ovation when he rolled the stone away and came back outside. When you get right down to it, this is another betrayal.

Postscript to Jesus Is Back: It's really weird that the resurrection of Jesus is without question the single most important event in the entire Bible and it gets a single paragraph of coverage in each of the four gospels—that's it—and none of the gospels agrees on who came to the tomb and discovered that the body of Jesus was no longer there or frankly any of the details of the scene.

Here's the rundown:

Matthew: "Mary Magdalene and the other Mary" go to the tomb; there's an earthquake; an angel who looks like lightning descends from heaven, scares the guards, rolls away the stone from the tomb, sits on it and tells the two women that Jesus has risen from the dead and that they will find him in Galilee. The women leave and immediately run into Jesus, so they actually don't have to wait until they get to Galilee to see him, despite what the angel just said. Apparently Jesus is in a rather formal mood after rising from the dead since the first word out of his mouth when he sees the women is "Greetings!"

Mark: Three women, not two, go to the tomb: Mary Magdalene; Mary, the mother of James; and Salome. There's no earthquake. There's a young man inside the tomb. He is not described as looking like lightning, and there are no guards for him to scare. He tells the three women that Jesus has risen and that they will find him in Galilee. They do not encounter Jesus after leaving the tomb. They are described as "afraid."

Luke: Unnamed women go to the tomb. The stone is rolled away, and Jesus is gone. There is no earthquake, and there are no guards. Two men "in dazzling apparel" tell the women that Jesus has risen. Later Mary Magdalene; Joanna; Mary, the mother of James; "and the other women with them" tell the apostles that Jesus has risen from the dead. The apostles do not believe them. However, Peter goes to the tomb by himself, and when he finds the tomb empty, he marvels "at what had happened."

John: Mary Magdalene goes to the tomb by herself and finds that the stone has been moved away from the tomb. There is no earthquake, no angel or angels and no guards. She finds Peter and John. She does not say that Jesus has risen from the dead. Instead she says, "They have taken the Lord out of the tomb, and we do not know where they have laid him." Peter and John go to the tomb, confirm that he is gone and return home. A weeping Mary Magdalene then encounters two angels in the tomb, who want to know why she is crying. She tells them she is crying because Jesus' body has been taken from the tomb, and she does not know where it is. Then she turns around, and Jesus is standing there, but she does not recognize him and thinks he is the gardener. When Jesus says her name, she instantly recognizes him, and we're told that she answers him "In Aramaic, 'Rabboni' (which means Teacher)."

To summarize: Maybe one woman or maybe a number of women—two, three, maybe more—go to the tomb of Jesus and find that his body is no longer there. There is or is not an earthquake. There may or may not be guards. An angel or a young man or two men or two angels are there. They may or may not say that Jesus has risen from the dead. Maybe Peter shows up, too, or maybe it's Peter and

John or maybe neither of them is there. Jesus appears, or maybe he doesn't. That's the story. Those are the descriptions that we have of what is supposedly the most important event ever to occur on the face of the earth—the resurrection of Jesus.

I wonder what the NYPD or the FBI would make of these conflicting accounts. I don't know. Maybe the Warren Commission could figure out what actually happened.

58

Heaven: Open for Business

I think about Elijah all alone for all those years in heaven. We're talking about something like 900 years all by himself. What did he do all day? I think about his fiery horses, too, and the fiery chariots. Did their fires go out?

You would think that Elijah would have been really happy when Jesus died and heaven was finally open for business. On the other hand, maybe he liked having heaven all to himself. Can you imagine living by yourself for years and years and then all of a sudden a few million people show up looking for dinner and some light entertainment?

Of course, this just raises the question, what do you do in heaven? I've never heard anybody come up with anything that sounds even a little bit interesting. It's always seemed to me that you'd be bored after about ten minutes. I've always imagined it as a kind of big waiting room where you never get in to see the doctor.

I'm not very satisfied at all with the idea that you just stare at God all of the time either. That's called the Beatific Vision. If that's what you do, I'm sorry, but I'm going to protest by keeping my eyes closed. I mean is God ever going to get over himself? If heaven is nothing but the face of God 24/7, I'm going to throw up.

The other thing I want to know is when Jesus opened up heaven and let all of the dead people from the Old Testament out of Sheol, what exactly were the criteria for deciding who went to heaven? You have to think since God authorized and enabled the Chosen People to slaughter everybody who was living in the Promised Land so that they could move in themselves, that you were not disqualified if you were a mass murderer. Child rape was also OK back then. I know one thing. Worshipping false gods would definitely disqualify you. Other than that, it's really hard to say. I guess you have to be God to figure it all out.

59

GOODBYE

I wonder what it looked like when Jesus ascended into heaven.
It's hard to imagine without Mary Poppins coming into your head.
Sometimes the Travelers insurance guy with the top hat and the big
red umbrella pops up, too.

Did a wind kick up, or did he suddenly levitate off the ground
and just keep going up? After he's off the ground, a cloud rolls up
and takes him away. What kind of a cloud was that? Was it white
and puffy or kind of all wispy? Was it just vapor, or was it a special
cloud with some kind of invisible floor?

I have the same problem here as I do with Elijah going up to
heaven. Did he disappear all of a sudden at some point, or did he
just keep going up and then just pass out of sight?

While Jesus is ascending, two guys who weren't there before
suddenly appear. They're dressed in robes, so I guess we're supposed to think they're angels. They tell the apostles to stop staring
at the sky. Don't worry. He'll be back, they say.

Mark says that as soon as Jesus got to heaven, he sat down at the
right hand of God. Everybody just sort of accepts this as though it
makes sense. I'd like to know why he sat down. Was he tired? Why
does he sit on the right hand of God instead of on the left? Why is

the left always bad and the right always, well, right? Is it possible that there was just a more comfortable chair on the right?

Finally what could that have looked like? Jesus sitting on the right hand of God—I mean Jesus is God, so he's actually sitting to the right of himself. How the heck do you do that? Sorry, but I just can't say, it's a mystery. I think I'll just admit I have no fucking idea.

60

THE HOLY SPIRIT

I've always felt that the Holy Spirit was kind of an embarrassment. Does anybody really think he's equal to God the Father and Jesus?

Imagine taking a family picture of the trinity. You have a fatherly God with a big beard, looking like the guy in the Oak Ridge Boys in the middle. Then you have Jesus looking a little bit like Johnny Depp at the Golden Globes, and then on the left you have what? Is it a bird, something like a dove? Maybe then the photographer would tell him to sit on Jesus' shoulder. Or do you have a divided tongue of fire or lots of tongues of fire flaming away? I can tell you from girls I know that a divided tongue can be sexy with the right jewelry, but it at least needs to be in somebody's mouth.

The problem is if you catch the Holy Spirit on a day when he's just a big wind blowing through and you try to take a picture, it's going to look like he's missing. Like maybe God the Father and Jesus were embarrassed about the situation, too, and they gave him the wrong time for the photo shoot.

61

THE APOSTLES

The apostles are not a very impressive group of guys. It's true that they don't get much play in the Gospels, but the little that we do see of them shows that they're a rag tag bunch of fair weather friends. They don't seem that bright either. They have a hard time understanding the parables even though they're supposedly hip to the code. Judas betrays Jesus; Peter denies him; when Jesus is arrested, they all scatter and hide; none of them are there for him when he's crucified except maybe John, but that's only in the account by whoever wrote the Gospel of John, and maybe he was just standing up for his namesake. Finally they don't believe that he's risen from the dead even though he repeatedly told them that he would do that.

At a certain point you wonder a little bit about Jesus' judgment in picking these guys. If he were an NFL general manager and he had a draft this bad, he'd be fired.

Postscript to The Apostles: Actually you really have to wonder about these guys from the very beginning. One day, totally out of the blue, Jesus stops by where the brothers, Peter and Andrew, are fishing, and he says to them, "Follow me, and I will make you fishers of men." Immediately they abandon their jobs and go off with a total stranger. Two other brothers, James and John, do the same exact thing. So does Matthew, the tax collector. This is always presented as some great thing that the apostles do—some great evidence of their faith. Actually it's completely nuts. Can you imagine anybody doing this today? A total stranger walks by the cubicle next to yours, says "Follow me," to your co-worker, and he gets up and walks out the door never to be seen again. Wow! I wonder how the apostles' families felt about having been abandoned and having been left with no means of support. I wonder how many children were involved here, too.

62

THE CONVERT

Beware of the convert. If you see him coming your way, run. There's nothing worse than being cornered by a guy who's fanatically opposed to everything he used to do. It doesn't matter if he was into alcohol or drugs or smoking or sex or jaywalking, conversion turns that happy go lucky guy you used to step over at parties to get to the fridge into a cold-blooded fanatic. A zealot. The guy who used to say yes to everything is now the guy who has definitely learned to just say no, and he's dedicated himself to making sure that everybody else on the planet says no, too.

Now in this case we're not talking about a guy who's going from wet to dry, smoky to smoke free or whore master to choirmaster. It's more like persecutor to proselytizer. We're talking here about the Apostle Paul. The first time we see him, he's the coat check guy for the crowd that's stoning to death Stephen, the first Christian martyr. I hope they tipped him well. Next thing you know, he's struck by a blinding light from heaven and knocked off his horse while traveling on the road to Damascus. From that moment on, all of the cold, furious energy that he poured into dragging people out of their homes and imprisoning them, all of the fervor that he devoted to persecution and execution is turned toward spreading the Good News of Jesus throughout the world.

I have to give Paul credit. He's literally all over the map. From Damascus to Jerusalem to Cyprus to Macedonia to Athens to Corinth to Ephesus to Rome, Paul is out there risking life and limb to witness to the truth.

After the death and resurrection and ascension of Jesus, the rest of the New Testament is pretty much all by and about Paul. It's pushing it a little bit, but you could make the argument that Paul's spin on Jesus' teaching has had as big an impact on how Christianity has been taught and practiced as Jesus himself.

63

PAUL IS THE GUY

Paul is the guy who turns Jesus into a religion, institutional, that is.

Paul is the guy who dreams up original sin.

Paul is the guy who says forget about good works because we're all so sinful and fallen we aren't capable of good works anyway.

Paul is the guy who says doing good works is not how you're saved. It's through the free grace of Our Lord Jesus Christ. That is what allows a worthless human sinner to accept Jesus Christ as Lord and savior and be born again. (Note: If the number of hypocritical words and actions spawned by this one idea could ever be calculated, it would certainly exceed the number of subatomic particles in the universe.)

To continue:

Paul is the guy who proclaims sex "icky."

Paul is the guy who says we should all remain subject to the governing authorities and rulers because their authority comes from God. (So much for the American Revolution and the Civil Rights Movement.)

Paul is the guy who sanctions slavery.

Paul is the guy who puts women in their place.

Paul is the guy who demonizes homosexuality.

No doubt about it. Paul is definitely the guy.

64

Message from Paul: Sex Is Dirty

There is a perverse pleasure in finding out who the guy was who made you feel guilty when you were 12 years old and your dick got hard. That guy would be Paul. Message to Paul—I got over it.

Paul thought that sex was dirty, but he was wrong. Sex is not always dirty. It's only dirty when it's good. When it's bad, it's anything but dirty. It's an obligation to procreate, or maybe it's a habit. It's whatever. It's what stops when the relationship goes south.

Paul doesn't know any of this. Maybe he had a really bad experience with a hooker before his conversion. Maybe he had ED in the days before Viagra. I don't know. Whatever the explanation, Paul is positively creepy in his attitude toward sex.

Paul thinks that sex should only happen in marriage and then only for the purpose of procreation. Ideally each of the guilty parties should have a pained look on their faces as if they're passing a kidney stone or a really hard, constipated stool. Apparently Paul didn't know that marriage is the end of sex. Of course, if he had known that, he would have recommended that everybody get married. Instead he gives the following advice: "I wish that all were as I myself am," i.e., single and celibate. "To the unmarried and the widows I say that it is good to remain single as I am. But if they cannot exercise self-control, they should marry. For it is better to marry than to burn with passion."

Translated: If you're not married and don't need sex, stay single. If you absolutely have to have sex at least once in your life, get married.

Whatever you say, Paul. Whatever you say.

65

SLAVERY: THE BIBLE MAN'S BURDEN

Paul supports slavery. He actually returns a slave, Onesimus, to his owner, Philemon. The guy gets away, and Paul sends him back. He does write a letter to Philemon in which he asks him to set Onesimus free, but in sending him back and leaving the decision up to Philemon, the slave owner, he's sanctioning the institution of slavery.

Paul also feels that it is his responsibility to instruct slaves in proper slave behavior and etiquette. Sorry, but I kind of think that Jesus was against slavery. He didn't say anything about it, but I have a hunch of what his position must be. I think he'd at least sign a petition.

Anyway can you imagine Jesus preaching on how to be a good slave? Paul has no problem providing instructions on this topic. He says that a good slave should "be submissive to their own masters in everything; they are to be well-pleasing not argumentative, not pilfering but showing all good faith, so that in everything they may adorn the doctrine of God our Savior."

Apparently slavery is the boutonniere on the lapel of God's plan for creation.

Postscript to Slavery: The Catholic Church made Philemon, the slave owner, and Onesimus, the slave, both saints. Philemon's feast day is February 19. The feast day of Onesimus is February 16. The Lutheran Church-Missouri Synod also made Onesimus and Philemon saints. They have a day set aside, February 15, to celebrate both of them. Holy slave owner. Holy slave. That's a match made in heaven.

66

THE BIBLE AND WOMEN

God thinks that women should be subordinate to men. First of all he made Eve from Adam's rib, so it stands to reason that a woman would be worth less than a man. After the fiasco in the garden, he also made Adam Eve's boss. You can also throw in the fact that men get to impregnate women and walk away, while women are left with the excruciating pain of childbirth.

There are many examples throughout the Bible of the subordination of women. Here are some of them:

God actually tells Moses how he values men and women comparatively in monetary terms. Here's the break down:

- Men from the ages of twenty to sixty are worth fifty shekels of silver; women of the same age group are worth thirty shekels; over sixty years old, it's 15 shekels for men and ten shekels for women.

- Boys from the age of five to twenty are worth twenty shekels; girls of that age group are worth ten shekels.

- Boys from a month old up to the age of five are worth five shekels, while girls of that age group are worth three shekels.

Apparently babies under a month old aren't worth anything whether they're male or female.

If a man takes an oath, it stands, and he is bound by it. If a woman takes an oath, for good or ill, it can be voided by her father or her husband.

Women must remain virgins until they are given away by their fathers to a man in marriage—whether they like the guy or not; men can have multiple wives while maintaining mistresses and fucking prostitutes.

As noted previously, a father can also sell his daughter into slavery, so a girl really needs to watch her step around her father.

Women are held in such contempt that when the super-fratricidal Abimelech is mortally wounded by a rock dropped on his head by a woman, he tells his male armor bearer to draw his sword and kill him "lest they say of me, 'a woman killed him.'" Needless to say the armor bearer is only too happy to fulfill Abimelech's request.

In the New Testament, Paul delivers a litany of pronouncements asserting the subordination of women:

- "The head of a wife is a husband."

- "Wives, submit to your own husbands, as to the Lord. For the husband is the head of the wife even as Christ is the head of the church . . . Now also as the church submits to Christ so also wives should submit in everything to their husbands."

- "A man ought not to cover his head, since he is the image and glory of God, but woman is the glory of man, for man was not made from woman but woman from man. Neither was man created for woman but woman for man. That is why a wife ought to have a symbol of authority on her head."

OK. But I'm still trying to figure out why the symbol of authority over women is a head covering or hat. And are all hats the same as symbols of authority over women, or might there be differences? For example, is a top hat more powerful as a symbol of authority than a bowler or a beanie? Might the reverse be true? What about a Panama hat? How powerful is that? And, furthermore, are hoodies allowed?

- "The women should keep silent in the churches. For they are not permitted to speak but should be in submission, as the Law also says. If they should desire to learn, they should ask their husbands at home. For it is shameful for a woman to speak in church."

In this passage Paul is crystal clear. He says, "Women, if you're in church, shut the fuck up!" There is pretty clearly a question about whether women would typically have a desire to learn anything. If they should desire to learn (italics mine), they can ask their husbands at home, where presumably the answer will come from behind closed doors.

Now if you can't even open your mouth when you're in church, it's pretty much impossible for you to do anything but listen to the men. You certainly cannot be in a leadership position at all. Paul makes this painfully clear as well. He says, "Let a woman learn quietly in all submissiveness. I do not permit a woman to teach or to exercise authority over a man; rather, she is to remain quiet. For

Adam was formed first, then Eve; and Adam was not deceived, but the woman was deceived and became a transgressor. Yet she will be saved by child-bearing." So according to the natural order of things, women are gullible and easily deceived. They therefore need to yield to men, who are wiser and worldlier, and dedicate themselves to earning salvation by pumping out babies.

So that is the story about women, as far as Paul is concerned, and if women don't like it, too bad. He would simply say that these are not his rules. He's just doing his job, communicating God's laws about their place in creation. Blame God. Don't blame him. Interestingly, this is the very same argument that religious people make today when they assert that women must remain subordinate to men. They're not bigots, they say. They're not misogynists. They're just following the Bible.

67

THE BIBLE AND HOMOSEXUALITY

No doubt about it. God is anti-gay. In Leviticus 18:22 he says
"You shall not lie with a male as with a woman; it is an abomination." In fact, as I mentioned, if a man has sex with a man, they
both need to be executed. Interestingly, this passage from Leviticus
also gives you a pretty good clue as to why Rick Santorum was happy to talk about man on man and dog on dog in the same breath.
The very next verse, Leviticus 18:23, says, "And you shall not lie
with any animal and so make yourself unclean with it, neither shall
any woman give herself to an animal to lie with it: it is perversion."
How's that for guilt by association?

In the Old Testament, there is no mention by God, Moses or
anybody else about woman on woman, so you might think that
there's a loophole, and maybe it's OK with God to be a lesbian. But
I doubt it. Although God does take the time to tell women to stay
away from animals, there probably is no ban on lesbian sex because
women are viewed as men's property, men's chattel. They have no
rights and aren't worth mentioning. In any event leave it to Paul
to rectify this oversight. In his Letter to the Romans, he condemns
homosexuality and doesn't leave out the women. In describing the
ungodly and the unrighteous people who have worshipped false
gods he says that because of this betrayal, "God gave them up to
dishonorable passions. For their women exchanged natural rela-

tions for those that are contrary to nature; and the men likewise gave up natural relations with women and were consumed with passion for one another committing shameless acts with men and receiving the due penalty for their error."

That "due penalty" would be hell. Paul wants to send all gay people to hell. And I do have to hand it to him for hitting on something big here. Sending gay people to hell is a really popular idea right up to this very day. Some ideas just have a special appeal that crosses generations and unites multitudes of people from all sorts of nationalities and backgrounds. Whether you're rich or poor, old or young, black, white, yellow, brown or red, you may find that the idea of sending gay people to hell has an irresistible attraction and charm.

And you know what's best about hopping on the anti-gay bandwagon? You have the Bible to back you up.

68

HELL

What a concept! Hell. If you're bad or God doesn't like you for some reason, he sends you to hell, and you stay there forever. Back in the Old Testament everybody went to Sheol. As I've noted, Sheol was a big deep, dark hole in the ground, a mass grave. That doesn't sound very inviting. It makes me think of Edgar Allen Poe and "The Premature Burial" or Joe Pesci digging his own grave in Casino.

When you went to Sheol, you turned into something called a shade, sort of like a ghost, and you could be called up by a medium the way Samuel was if somebody had a question about something. If you were a prophet, you might get a question about the future. The good thing, too, was that eventually, if you were on the invitation list, you were promoted to heaven. You had to wait until Jesus came and died for everybody's sins. Somehow killing his own Son made God the Father feel better about everybody's sins. He loves sacrifices, and once Jesus came down and took one for the team, he opened up heaven for business.

The problem, of course, was that you might not be on the invitation list to get into heaven. You might be on the other list—the list that entitles you to a one-way ticket to hell for eternity. That is the place, of course, of eternal fire. It is "the fiery furnace" where the damned burn forever and "their worm does not die." It makes going to Sheol seem like a typical day in the high school detention hall.

After Jesus was crucified, he shut down Sheol and opened up heaven and hell. It was as if he had two Grand Openings on the same day. I wonder what the attendance was at each opening on Day One? Did more people go to heaven, or did more people go to hell? What was the proportion between the two?

We're talking about a lot of people. Sheol was one crowded place. An awful lot of shades were packed into that hole. The best estimates are fairly speculative on how many people would have lived and died by the time Jesus died on the cross, but we're in the neighborhood of about 46 billion people if we start counting from about 50,000 BC and assume 80 births per 1,000 people per year.

Of course, nobody knows the answer to my question. But people do try to come up with numbers. Just Google the question, and you'll be treated to a really entertaining carnival ride into mindless malevolence and absurdity. I think it's funny that a lot of fundamentalist believers think that almost everybody who has died is in hell but that they and their co-believers, i.e., those who are in the same religious group or cult as they, the ones who sit in the same pew with them, so to speak, are all in the tiny minority who are going to heaven. Isn't that special? Actually that's another problem I have with heaven. I have no interest in hanging out with most of the people who think they're going to wind up there.

Now when it comes to trying to figure out how many people are in hell, we're just talking, of course, about this planet. I'll have a panic attack if I try to start calculating how many intelligent life forms on all of the other inhabited planets—maybe billions of planets—have also ended up in hell. Hey, maybe the total number of people in hell, the total number of the damned is—googol!

A final point: I think it reflects rather badly on God that he would create a universe in which almost all of the people and all of the other intelligent life forms end up in hell—especially since he's supposed to know that this is going to happen even before he creates the universe. What exactly was he thinking? If you set a bar that almost nobody clears, there's something wrong with the bar. If you make rules that almost nobody follows, there's something wrong with the rules.

Also, why hell? Why that punishment? Burning in a fire for eternity? That's your idea of a just punishment? Really? Why not just some form of community service?

By the way, don't bother making the free-will argument. That's the argument made by that tiny cult minority that thinks they're among the precious few who are saved. We've seen that God suspends free will whenever he wants. Also, there can be no capacity for evil that does not also exist in the creator.

Almost everybody goes to hell? I just think it's mean. That's all.

69

THE OLD TESTAMENT GOD VS. THE NEW TESTAMENT GOD

No way around it. The Old Testament God and the New Testament God seem to be two different guys. They both go by the name of God, but they just don't seem to be the same guy. Now we know the OT God's MO. We've gone through all of the horrific things he's done: Adam and Eve eat a piece of fruit that God tells them not to eat, and in response he invents suffering and death and imposes them on everybody else who will ever live; lots of people are behaving badly, so God kills everybody, except for Noah and his family and several million very lucky animals and insects; he decides the people of Israel are his favorites, and he massacres anybody who happens to be living where he wants his people to live, and so on and so forth.

Now that's just not the same God that we find in the New Testament. No way, not even close—whether we're talking about God, the Father; God, the Son—that would be Jesus; or God, the Holy Spirit. When Jesus gets baptized by John, and the Spirit comes down like a dove and a voice says, "This is my beloved Son, with whom I am well pleased," we know we're in a whole new ball game. The dove adds a very gentle feeling to the whole scene. You might even say, lovey-dovey. And every time I think about that voice from heaven saying how much he loves his Son and how pleased he is with him, I think of Ward on Leave It to Beaver or Fred McMurray on My Three Sons.

Should we consider the possibility that God has evolved? I thought that God was supposed to be eternal and unchanging. You know how he always was, always will be, and always remains the same. That's how the Baltimore Catechism describes him. Maybe he is the same behind the scenes, but he just relates differently in the New Testament. His Son is down on earth, working miracles and healing the sick but kicking up lots of trouble, too, and he knows that it's going to end badly, and it's like he's there looking out the window of heaven all worried and waiting for Jesus to come home. Maybe he's just as mean, but he seems softer because he's worried about his Son. We all know people like that, like if you have an abusive father and then when you have kids, he's all mellowed out and cuddly with them. You want to say, "Hey, Pop, if you're so nice now, why'd you always beat the shit out of me?" You know the guy is still a prick, but there he is on the floor playing with little baby Joey.

One thing we do know though. God has gotten a lot more elusive. Back in the glory days when the Chosen People were lost in the desert, he used to show up all of the time. He'd talk to Moses just about every day, and he was always sending down fire or opening up the earth to kill anybody who got out of line. Now when he talks to people, nobody else is ever around to see him or hear him, too. To give you just one example, Michele Bachmann says that God speaks to her all of the time. She prays, and God speaks back. If these talks are so frequent, why couldn't she have at least had Fox News come by on the day that God told her she should run for president? In retrospect, though, you have to wonder if God was just fucking with Michele given how well that worked out for her.

70

UNANSWERED QUESTIONS

I have a lot of questions about stuff from the Bible, and unfortunately I have serious doubts about whether I'll ever get an answer to any of these questions. I've asked a few already. For example, there must be a reason why Lot's wife was turned into a pillar of salt and not some other condiment, but I don't know what it is. Also, I don't think anybody knows where God's sons, including Satan, came from. How did he have sons, and who was their mother? Here are some additional questions that I just can't find answers to:

It Rained for Forty Days and Forty Nights: Let's start with a question that has an answer. I just don't know what it is. If it rained for forty days and forty nights at the North and South Poles, what would the effect be on the polar icecaps?

God Wrestles Jacob: What possessed God to wrestle all night with Jacob, especially since it turns out that Jacob is at least as good a wrestler as God? They wrestled all night, and God couldn't beat him. Or are we supposed to think that God threw the match? Does anybody else think that it was sort of cheating when God saw that he wasn't going to win fair and square and drew on some special supernatural power to dislocate Jacob's hip by just touching it?

Flat Tax: When God tells Moses to impose a census tax on the people of Israel, he says, "Everyone who is numbered in the census, from twenty years old and upward, shall give the Lord's offering. The rich shall not give more, and the poor shall not give less, than the half shekel, when you give the Lord's offering to make atonement for your lives." Question: Does this mean that God supports the flat tax?

Test for Adultery: Back in Moses' time, if you suspected your wife of cheating on you, God had devised a test that would show whether she did or not. You brought your wife over to the priest along with some barley flour. The priest took the barley flour, put some water in a pot, threw some dust into the water, made your wife hold the barley flour and drink the water with the dust in it. Then he made her swear before God that she would be cursed if she cheated on you. Then he took the barley flour from your wife and did some fancy priestly actions with it, like waving it around and burning some of it on the altar. Then he made your wife drink the dusty water again. If she had not cheated on you, she was fine, but if she had cheated, her uterus would swell up and her thigh would "fall away." I'm not sure what it means for her thigh to fall away, but it can't be good. By the way, God never devised a test to prove whether or not a husband had cheated on his wife. I doubt that there even was such a concept. A few questions: Has anybody tried this test to see if it still works? Is it available online? Do you get your money back if it doesn't work?

The Sun Stops: This is a little bit confusing. With God's help, we are told that Joshua makes the sun stop in its orbit around the earth on the day that God enables the Chosen People to defeat the

Amorites. The moon stands still as well. Sunset is delayed for the better part of a day, and we are told that "there has been no day like it before or since." Question: What would Galileo have thought about this passage?

The Judgment of Solomon: We all know the famous story of how Solomon was able to identify the real mother when two women came to him claiming to be the mother of the same baby. He tells them that he'll divide the baby between them by cutting it in half. The real mother is horrified and tells Solomon to give the baby to the other woman, while the false mother says fine, cut away. I'll take half a baby. We all know the story because most of us heard it at Sunday school or in some Bible study class when we were kids. Well, I bet most people don't know that the two mothers are both prostitutes. That part of the story is usually left out, censored. Question: Why is it OK for kids to hear that a baby might be cut in half, but it's not OK for them to know that the mommies are both hookers?

Solomon's Proverbs Against Adultery: Solomon had 700 wives and 300 concubines. He also wrote proverbs against adultery. My question is simple: What was he thinking? Actually, I have one more question. He addressed the proverbs to his son. Was the boy's mother one of the 700 wives or one of the 300 concubines? Solomon doesn't say.

The Death of Ahab: In a battle against the Syrians, King Ahab got killed in his chariot, and his blood ended up in a pool at the bottom of the chariot. After the battle, Ahab and his chariot were brought to Samaria, where he was buried. It was then that they finally got around to washing the chariot. We're told it was also then that dogs licked up his blood, just as Elijah had predicted. We're also told that prostitutes washed in his blood. My question is this: How does any of this make sense? The blood would have been dried for a long time, but dogs are licking it, and prostitutes are somehow in there washing in the dried blood and all the while some poor guys are trying to clean the blood off the chariot. All I can say is, help! If somebody can clear up what's going on here, I would really appreciate it. Sometime later, Ahab's wife Jezebel is thrown out of a window, and her body is eaten by dogs, but I have no problem with that because it seems that the dogs ate her right away, maybe even as soon as she hit the ground, and no prostitutes showed up to complicate matters.

Jonah in the Belly of the Fish: Can anybody tell me if there is any other example in all of human history of a person being eaten by a fish and surviving? What fish would that be? Similarly, is there an example of anybody ever being eaten by a whale and surviving? There seems to be some confusion over whether Jonah was eaten by a fish or a whale, but there is no disagreement over the fact that he survived. He lived for three days in the stomach of the fish or the whale, and he kept praying the whole time that he was in there, and then at the end of the three days, God told the fish or the whale to let Jonah go, and the fish or the whale vomited, and he landed on a shore and lived to tell the tale. Did that ever happen to anybody else anywhere? If it did and you know about it, please fill me in.

The Wise Men: Why were the Wise Men called "wise men"? They must all have known something or done something that made them wise. What was it? Also, it seems that they somehow got word from somebody that a star would lead them to where Jesus was born, but how did they get the message and how did they end up going together? Were they all at the same party when the message came? Also, how many Wise Men were there? Everybody thinks there were three, but that's just because there were three gifts, the famous gold, frankincense and myrrh. Maybe only three of them brought gifts, and the other guys stiffed Jesus. Maybe they thought that just showing up was enough.

One More Question About the Wise Men: If the Wise Men were so smart, why is it that they had a star to guide them to Bethlehem where Jesus was born, but they ended up in Jerusalem asking for directions? In fact, they make such a fuss over being lost, that King Herod finds out they're looking for the baby who will grow up to be the King of the Jews, and he hauls them into the palace for a secret meeting. Amazingly, Herod is the one who ends up giving them directions. He gathers together all of his priests and scribes and asks them where the new King of the Jews is supposed to be born. They tell him Bethlehem, and Herod sends the Wise Men there. He tells them that when they find the baby, they should let him know so that he can come and worship him, too. Right. Anyway when they're back on the road, they find that their GPS is working again. The star appears, and they finally follow it to Jesus' house. Now apparently the gullible Wise Men were actually ready to go back to Jerusalem on their way home and tell King Herod where the little baby Jesus was, but fortunately they are all warned by the same dream that it's probably not a good idea. As a result, they take an alternate route back. I'm disappointed to report that there is no word on whether they got lost again trying to take that different road home.

Joseph—What in the World Happened to Him? After the story about Jesus leaving his parents without notice to preach in the temple, we never see Joseph again. What happened to him? Nobody has anything to say about it. He just vanishes. Wasn't what happened to Jesus' foster father important? I guess not.

Drinking: This question must have an answer, but I just don't know what it is. Since Jesus turned water into wine, he couldn't have been against drinking. Why are so many fundamentalist Christians against it? Is it because John the Baptist didn't drink?

71

REVELATION

Revelation is a trip. If you want to understand it, I suggest you first read the collected works of Edward Lear and Lewis Carroll and play a lot of Beatles songs backwards.

I don't want to get all caught up in my underwear right here when I'm ready to wrap up, so I'll just cut to the chase and check out who's in the house at John's Apocalypse Lounge.

Actually it's pretty crowded tonight. The bartender is an angel, a white haired dude, and as usual he's wearing a golden sash around his chest. That's his trademark. You've got the angels of the churches in Ephesus, Smyrna, Pergamum, Thyatira, Sardis, Philadelphia and Laodicea all sitting together at a table off to the side. In a banquet room in the back are 24 elders along with the four living creatures—a lion, an ox, the face of a man and an eagle in flight. The living creatures will be performing an acoustic set later tonight.

At a table all by itself is a bloody lamb with seven horns and seven eyes staring at a scroll with seven seals. The lamb looks like it's definitely on something, and everybody's giving it plenty of space.

All of a sudden a whole other bunch of angels come through the door and go straight to the bar and send drinks over to the table of the angels of the seven churches. Nice.

Now it's starting to get packed. The place is just crawling with angels. I can't even keep up with everybody who's here. For some reason a lot of the angels have trumpets. I can also pick out four cowboys or horsemen at a table in the back, a pregnant woman sitting by herself, and two crazy-looking beasts sitting together. One has ten horns and seven heads and the other one looks like a sheep or a lamb that's been in a really bad car accident.

I like hanging out at bars with a pretty good mix of clientele. Usually I'll click with somebody, and we'll have a drink and chill out together for a while. Sometimes somebody will come up to me and say hi, how've you been? It's been a long time, and I'll have no idea who they are, no memory at all of ever meeting them. Weird.

Anyway I'm beginning to think that it just isn't going to happen tonight. I'm about to leave when I see her. She's "arrayed in purple and scarlet and adorned with gold and jewels and pearls, holding in her hand a golden cup full of abominations." It's the Great Prostitute. Sometimes she goes by the name of the Whore of Babylon. I know her from a couple of late nights at the Heart Bar in Vegas.

The Genesis of *You Got to Be Kidding!*

The genesis of my book, *You Got to Be Kidding! A Radical Satire of The Bible*, is kind of strange. I woke up one morning, and the first thing I thought of was that I would read the Bible and when I found something funny, I would write about it. I had never had that thought before, and I don't know why I woke up thinking the Bible was funny, although it is hilarious.

I went over to my kitchen table, sat down at my laptop and downloaded an electronic version of the Bible. I read it until I got to the Adam and Eve story, and then I wrote the first sketch of the book. Over the next several weeks I read the Bible and wrote more than 70 satirical sketches. I wrote them really fast like a bunch of emails, hardly changing a word.

So that's how I wrote the book. But why did I write it? I wrote it for two closely related reasons. First of all, I wanted to expose the absurdity of the Bible. How is the Bible absurd? Well, the most absurd thing about the Bible is that in all probability almost nothing of importance described in it ever actually happened.

What else? How about Mosaic Law, Old Testament morality? It's not really morality at all. It's more like tribal code. Like, if you do work on the Sabbath, you should be stoned to death or, if you're a woman and you pretend to be a virgin and then you get married, your husband can have you stoned to death for having fibbed about being a virgin—that sort of thing. Funny, when I think of who today best embodies the values of Old Testament morality, it's really the Taliban.

Then, of course, there's Leviticus, 18:22, "You shall not lie with a male as with a woman; it is an abomination." During Rick Santorum's campaign for the Republican nomination for president, reporters discovered that a few years earlier, he had said that "the definition of marriage" has never "included homosexuality. That's not to pick on homosexuality. It's not, you know, man on child, man on dog, or whatever the case may be." Some people were shocked that Santorum had equated homosexuality with bestiality. Actually it isn't surprising at all. Right after Leviticus 18:22 calls homosexuality an abomination, the very next verse says, "And you shall not lie with any animal." Wow! Smoking gun!

That brings me to the second reason why I wrote the book, and I'm very passionate about this. Bigots use the Bible all the time to justify their bigotry against gay and transgender people. They also use it to defend the subordination of women to men. These people say the Bible is the inspired word of God. Right. The Creator of the Universe is the real author of the Bible. How's that for absurd! But if you believe that God inspired the Bible, then if you hate gay and transgender people, you can certainly say that God is on your side because the Bible is definitely anti-gay—not just the Old Testament but the New Testament too. The Old Testament is actually pretty easy on gay people by comparison. It just wants them dead, but the

New Testament goes further. It says that, if you're gay, once you're dead, you should go to hell and burn in a fire forever and ever.

So the Bible-believing haters do have a point. The Bible, the inspired word of God, is hateful toward gay and transgender people, but that doesn't impress me. I say just because God is a bigot doesn't make it right.

We all need to stand up against people who use the Bible and religion to justify their own hatred and bigotry. My book does it with satirical humor. It's the humor of what I call a Cultural Arsonist, a person dedicated to setting fire to stupidity and burning up bigotry—metaphorically, that is. My book shows that if you have a radical sense of humor and you read the Bible literally, you get satire rather than fundamentalism. You get skepticism rather than blind faith. You get humor versus hatred.

In fact, what you get is my book, You Got to Be Kidding!

ABOUT THE AUTHOR

DR. JOE WENKE is an outspoken and articulate LGBTQ rights activist, social critic and observational satirist. He is the founder and publisher of Trans Über, a publishing company with a focus on promoting LGBTQ rights, free thought and equality for all people.

In addition to *YOU GOT TO BE KIDDING! A Radical Satire of The Bible,* Wenke is the author of *PAPAL BULL: An Ex-Catholic Calls Out the Catholic Church, THE TALK SHOW,* a novel, and *MAILER'S AMERICA.* He also partners with Gisele Xtravaganza in Gisele New World, which produces events for the ballroom community. Wenke received a B.A. in English from the University of Notre Dame, an M.A. in English from Penn State and a Ph.D. in English from the University of Connecticut. He is also a frequent contributor to the Huffington Post.

Author's photo by Gisele Xtravaganza